Optavia Diet Cookbook

250+ Healthy, Easy, And Super Energetic Recipes to Reset Your Metabolism and Lose Weight Fast.

Rebecca Falls

© Copyright 2021 - All rights reserved.

The content contained within this book may not be reproduced, duplicated or transmitted without direct written permission from the author or the publisher.

Under no circumstances will any blame or legal responsibility be held against the publisher, or author, for any damages, reparation, or monetary loss due to the information contained within this book. Either directly or indirectly.

Legal Notice:

This book is copyright protected. This book is only for personal use. You cannot amend, distribute, sell, use, quote or paraphrase any part, or the content within this book, without the consent of the author or publisher.

Disclaimer Notice:

Please note the information contained within this document is for educational and entertainment purposes only. All effort has been executed to present accurate, up to date, and reliable, complete information. No warranties of any kind are declared or implied. Readers acknowledge that the author is not engaging in the rendering of legal, financial, medical or professional advice. The content within this book has been derived from various sources. Please consult a licensed professional before attempting any techniques outlined in this book.

By reading this document, the reader agrees that under no circumstances is the author responsible for any losses, direct or indirect, which are incurred as a result of the use of information contained within this document, including, but not limited to, errors, omissions, or inaccuracies.

Table of Contents

Introduction 5
CHAPTER 1: Optavia Diet Basics 6
   Beginning Phase 6
   The Principles of Optavia Diet 7
CHAPTER 2: The Benefits of Optavia Diet 8
   Easy to Follow 8
   May Improve Blood Pressure 8
   It Offers Continuous Support 9
   Achieves Fast Weight Loss 9
   It Removes Guesswork 9
CHAPTER 3: What You Can Eat 10
   What Not to Eat 10
   How Often Can You Eat? 11
CHAPTER 4: The Differences Between Optavia Diet and Other Famous Diets 12
   The Different Phases 12
CHAPTER 5: Breakfast 13
   Cheeses Waffles 13
   Super-Food Scramble 13
   Healthier Scramble 14
   Fall Morning Omelet 14
   Perfect Savory Waffles 15
   Chicken Zucchini Noodles 15
   Eggless Scramble 16
   Parmesan Zucchini 17
   Creamy Cauliflower Soup 17
   Taco Zucchini Boats 18
   Chinese Style Scramble 19
   Pesto Zucchini Noodles 19
   Baked Cod & Vegetables 20
   Healthy Broccoli Salad 20
   Tomato Cucumber Avocado Salad 21
CHAPTER 6: Poultry 22
   Caesar Chicken Lettuce Wraps 22
   Chicken Fillets with Artichoke Hearts .. 22

Almond-Maple Chicken 23
Chicken Loaf 23
Buffalo Chicken Spaghetti Squash 24
Chicken Alfredo 24
Broccoli Chicken Dijon 25
Turkey Burgers 26
Grilled Marinated Chicken 26
Chicken Casserole 27
Chicken Saute 27
CHAPTER 7: Seafood 29
   Blackened Shrimps with Salad Lettuce 29
   Shrimp Cobb Salad 29
   Broccoli Kale Salmon Burgers 30
   Lemon-Garlic Scallops 30
   Shrimp Cucumber Salad 31
   Steamed White Fish Tacos 31
   Asparagus & Shrimp Stir Fry 32
   Shrimp Scampi 33
CHAPTER 8: Vegetables 34
   Taco Zucchini Boats 34
   Summer Vegetables 35
   Slow-Cooked Buttery Mushrooms 35
   Pan-Seared Cod 36
   Stir-Fried Brussels Sprouts and Carrots 36
   Falafel Bites 37
   Quick Lemon Pepper Salmon 37
   Steamed Zucchini-Paprika 38
   Delicious Zucchini Quiche 38
   Stir-Fried Eggplant 39
   Tomato Avocado Salad 40
   Tortellini in Red Pepper Sauce 40
   Quick Vegetable Kebabs 41
   Turkey Spinach Egg Muffins 41
   Savoy Cabbage with Coconut Cream Sauce 42
   Steamed Squash Chowder 42
CHAPTER 9: Salads 44

Prosciutto and Figs Salad ... 44
Garden Vegetables and Chickpeas Salad ... 44
Broccoli Salad Moroccan Style ... 45
Parsley Cheese Balls ... 45
Layered Dip ... 46
Avocado Chicken Salad ... 46
Tunisian Style Carrot Salad ... 47
Beef Taco Salad ... 47
Garden Salad with Oranges and Olives ... 48
North African Zucchini Salad ... 49
Spanish Salad ... 49
Parsley Couscous Salad ... 50
Grilled Tempeh Sticks ... 50
Avocado Salad ... 51
Peppered Watercress Salad ... 51
Caprese Salad ... 52
Caesar Salad ... 52
Cress and Tangerine Salad ... 53

CHAPTER 10: Sandwiches ... 54

White Bean Soup with Turkey Sausage and Kale ... 54
Chicken Salad Sandwiches ... 54
Avocado-Egg Salad Sandwich ... 55
Italian Sloppy Joe ... 55
Turkey Taco Lettuce Wraps ... 56
Tomato Finger Sandwich ... 57
Slow-cooker French Dip Sandwiches ... 57
Egg & Cheese Bagel Sandwich ... 58

CHAPTER 11: Lean Meat ... 59

Teriyaki Pork Stir-Fry ... 59
Adobo Sirloin ... 59
Asian Inspired Beef ... 60
Beef Stroganoff ... 61
Beef lo Mein ... 61
Mexican Beef Bowl ... 62
Weeknight Dinner Meal ... 63
Filling Beef Dish ... 64

CHAPTER 12: Optavia Recipes ... 65

Super-Delicious Avocado ... 65
Baked Chicken and Zucchini Casserole ... 65
Chicken Rice ... 66
Mexican Turkey Soup ... 66
Tuna Boats ... 67
Philly Cheesesteak Stuffed Peppers ... 67
Aromatic Chicken Platter ... 68
Attractive Scallop Salad ... 69
Pesto Zucchini Noodles with Grilled Chicken ... 69
Citrusy Fruit Salad ... 70
Italian Flair Chicken ... 71
Cauliflower and Chicken Tzatziki Bowl ... 71
Bibimbap Bowls ... 72
Chicken Fajita Platter ... 73
Broccoli Taco Bowl ... 73
Summertime Dinner Chicken ... 74
Authentic Chinese Chicken ... 74

CHAPTER 13: Fueling Recipes ... 76

Pumpkin Pie Trail Mix ... 76
Chocolate Popsicle ... 76
Tropical Chia Seed Pudding ... 77
Blueberry Muffins ... 77
Delicious Brownie Bites ... 78
Chocolate Bars ... 78
Coconut Colada ... 79
Dark Chocolate Berry Dessert Parfait ... 79
Vanilla Avocado Popsicles ... 79
Pumpkin Pie Frappe ... 80
Boo-Nila Shake ... 80
Chia Pudding ... 81
Richly Tasty Crepe ... 81
Peanut Butter Coconut Popsicle ... 82
Smooth Peanut Butter Cream ... 82
Avocado Pudding ... 82
Skinny Peppermint Mocha ... 83
Pumpkin Balls ... 83

Conclusion ... 84

Introduction

Before you dive into the book, let's give you a quick overview of the Optavia diet. There are three distinct diet plans that people who choose to adopt the Optavia diet program can select from. The variations differ in how many meals you will consume in a day and how many of them are pre-packaged as well as prepared by you at home. Consistent and reliable digital support is, hands down, one of the best things this program offers. In addition to the prepared meals, there are mentors, online help, and guidelines that gradually encourage the change of one habit at a time. Finally, the brand also offers services targeted at seniors and teens. If rapid weight loss is what you want, the Optavia diet could be a remedy.

This is most definitely the explanation of why it has gained so much momentum recently. Since the bulk of meals and snacks are pre-made, the diet can also seem smoother and more feasible. In addition to rapid weight reduction, the diet removes alcohol and sugar products, which, when taken in bulk, have clear links to chronic diseases. Desserts, including cookies, as well as most solid fats, like butter and coconut oil, are often prohibited. Finally, the program includes online access, weekly support sessions, and coaching for their online community. This may be an important aspect of progress in weight loss for many people.

While not everyone may want to sign up for a serious dieting regimen like this one, it does have its benefits, especially if you're looking to shed a few unneeded weights. So, these recipes have been prepared to serve as a holistic guide to everyone looking to start an effective Optavia diet. And if this is your first time getting to know about these recipes, we're delighted to introduce you to the world of Optavia diets; your dreams can actually come through; all you need to do is just follow closely.

Happy reading.

CHAPTER 1:
Optavia Diet Basics

The Optavia Diet offers users, like most meal-replacement programs, its own variety of packaged items that take over the role of many meals during the day. Optavia includes lifestyle plans with weight reduction and weight management targets. The other plans of Optavia, the "3&3" and "4&2&1," incorporate "real" meals with substitutes for meals. These deals are better for people who choose to steadily reduce weight or sustain their existing weight. Both "fueling" and "lean and green" prepared meals are kept inside tight calorie amounts on all Optavia schedules.

You begin by making a phone call with a trainer, irrespective of the plan you select, to help decide which Optavia plans to pursue, set targets for weight reduction, and acquaint oneself with the system.

The tagline of Optavia is "Lifelong Transition, One Healthy Habit at a Time." The main emphasis of the Optavia diet is a way of eating focuses on several mini-meals (called "Fuelings") eaten during the day, complemented by a home-cooked meal (termed "lean and green"). The program is built on six main optimum health building blocks:

- Weight Loss.
- Nutrition and Hydration.
- Motion.
- Sleeping.
- Your Mind.
- Your Environment.

The argument goes that you are less prone to wander into poor eating territories if you have a diet to follow and recommended mini-meals to consume. And weight reduction is almost assured because you just consume the small number of calories that the diet gives, even as little as 1,100 calories a day.

In comparison, balanced home cooking becomes a routine every night by planning your own "lean and green" meal, allowing the shift from the program back to "normal" healthier eating smoother.

Optavia also provides the aspect of social support that separates it from several other diets that substitute meals. As social support is a significant factor in the progress of weight reduction, those who participate in their services have access to a mentor, usually someone who has done the plan effectively. For your weight reduction path, this coach will address concerns, offer guidance, and act as a cheerleader.

Beginning Phase

Most people begin with the Optimal Weight 5&1 weight loss program, which is an 800–1,000 calorie routine said to help you lose 12 pounds over 12 weeks (5.4 kg). You consume 5 Optavia fuelings every day on this menu and 1 Lean and Green meal every day. You're expected to consume one meal every 2–3 hours and, on most days of the week, involve 30 minutes of a moderate workout. In sum, the fuelings and food focus on providing no more than 100 grams of carbohydrates per day. As Optavia trainers are compensated on commission, you purchase these fuelings from your trainer's specific page.

The aim of Lean and Green meals is to be rich in proteins and lighter in carbs. One meal contains 5–7 ounces of cooked lean protein (145–200 grams), three pieces of veggies, and up to 2 portions of good fats.

This schedule also involves one extra snack a day, which the coach would authorize. Three veggie sticks, 1/2 cup (60 grams) of sugar-free jelly, or 1/2 ounce (14 grams) of nuts are Plan-approved snacks. A dining-out guide that describes how to eat a Lean and Green meal at any favorite place is also included in the program. Please remember that the 5&1 Program actively prohibits alcohol.

The Principles of Optavia Diet

The developers of the Optavia Diet strive to be transparent when it comes to developing their many regimens and plans. But if you have questions about this diet regimen, then below are some FAQs that many people ask.

Which Optavia Diet Plan Is Good for Me?

As there are so many diet plans offered by Optavia, it is important to get in touch with a certified Optavia coach to learn about the many options that you have. It is crucial that you do not second guess the diet plan that you are going to follow, as each diet plan is designed to fit a particular profile. For instance, if you are a very active person, you can take on the Optavia 5&1 plan. But then, the coach will also look at other factors such as your age and health risks so that you can be matched with the right Optavia diet plan.

Can I Skip the Fuelings?

No. You must stick with fuelings if you want to successfully follow the Optavia diet. Fuelings are designed to provide the body with balanced amounts of macronutrients that can promote an efficient fat-burning state to help people lose fat without losing energy. The problem if you skip fueling is that you may miss out on important nutrients that might lead to fatigue while following this diet. The body feels fatigued because it cannot compensate for the lack of nutrients while being calorie deficient.

Can I Rearrange My Fuelings?

Yes. If you are a busy person with a dynamic schedule, then you can rearrange the timing on when you will take your fueling meals. The Optavia Diet is not strict about rearranging meals as long as you consume your meals within 24 hours. This versatility on your eating schedule makes it perfect for people who also have unusual schedules, including those who work at night or beyond regular working hours. So how do you time your fuelings? Just make sure that you eat your meals every two or three hours throughout the time that you are awake. Your first meal should be taken an hour after waking up to ensure optimal blood sugar levels. This is also great for hunger control.

CHAPTER 2:
The Benefits of Optavia Diet

Optavia diets encourage you to do away with junk by eating nutrition-rich fuelings and making your own food based on a healthy template. If you are often too busy to cook, the diet allows for a varying degree of flexibility when it comes to preparing your own meal, as well as a complementary degree of pre-packaged foods or fuelings to go with your cooking timetable. In essence, following the program is a no brainer as a structure has been provided for you. For individuals seeking to achieve weight loss through healthy eating, the recipes included serves just that purpose, but you're eating plan will depend on whether you're watching your weight or trying to reduce your weight. Whatever the case, the plans are simple and detailed. The coaching and community support help you adhere to the structure of the program.

In case you didn't know, the "Fuelings" are the features that make Optavia recipes stand out among many other weight loss programs. The fuelings are made without artificial additives, colors, or sweeteners. In addition to that, their "select" line is preservative-free. Although the meals are mostly pre-packaged, especially for the first two levels, they still do not contain any stimulants and no wacky pills or supplements. Emphasis is instead placed on regular eating of small portions of meals and snacks each day.

Previous studies by the team at Medifast showed that the Optavia diet might help improve blood pressure in obese people. This is due to the reduction in weight and reduced sodium intake. Research shows that high sodium levels aggravate the risk of high blood pressure in persons with underlying health conditions, especially salt-sensitive individuals. Optavia meal plans generally provide less than 2,300mg of sodium throughout the day. However, this may vary when it comes to the lean and green meals, in which case you're at liberty to choose between low and high sodium options. Additionally, the recipes are simple and easy to make, so you don't have to worry about spending too much time in the kitchen.

If you want a diet program that is simple and easy to execute, which can help you lose weight easily, and provides built-in support networks, Optavia's plan may be a good match for you.

Easy to Follow
Since the diet depends primarily on pre-packaged foods, on the 5&1 plan, you are only accountable for preparing one meal a day. What is more, to make things easy to execute, each schedule arrives with food journals and sample food choices. Although you are expected to prepare 1-3 Lean and Green recipes every day, they are quick to create based on the plan since the package provides unique recipes and a selection of choices for food. In addition, to supplement lean and green foods, many that are not interested in preparing can purchase prepared meals named "Flavors of Home."

May Improve Blood Pressure
Via weight loss and decreased sodium intake, Optavia plans may help improve blood pressure. Although the Optavia diet has not been extensively studied, a 40-week report on a related Medifast regimen in 90 individuals with extra weight or obesity showed a substantial decrease in blood pressure. In addition, all Optavia meal plans are planned to have less than 2,300 milligrams of sodium a day, but it is up to you to use low sodium Lean and Green meal alternatives. Numerous health associations recommend drinking fewer than 2,300 mg of sodium a day, including the American Heart Association, College of Medicine, and the United States

Department of Agriculture (USDA). That's because greater sodium consumption in sensitive populations is correlated with an elevated risk of hypertension and heart failure.

It Offers Continuous Support

For each weight-reduction plan, social support is a critical component of progress. The coaching service and community calls from Optavia include built-in motivation and customer assistance. All throughout weight reduction and maintenance plans, Optavia's fitness trainers are available. Specifically, one analysis identified an important association between the amount of Optavia 5&1 Strategy coaching sessions and enhanced weight loss. In addition, evidence shows that long-term weight management can be facilitated by obtaining a health coach or therapist. Coaching and community help is always excellent. Optavia provides coaching assistance and internet forums, video calls, and group meetings on a weekly basis. Training can be completely virtual, both digitally and by phone, but Optavia has a collection of coaches identified by area if you want to speak with a trainer in person.

Achieves Fast Weight Loss

In order to sustain their weight, most stable individuals consume about 1600 to 3000 calories a day. For certain individuals, reducing the amount to as little as 800 calories effectively ensures weight reduction. The 5&1 strategy of Optavia is meant for accelerated weight loss, making it a strong choice for those with a legitimate excuse to easily shed pounds.

It Removes Guesswork

Some people learn that the most daunting aspect of healthy eating is the emotional work needed to find out what to consume every day or even every dinner. Optavia alleviates the burden of meal preparation and "decision fatigue" by delivering "Fuelings" and "lean and green" menu suggestions to users for clear-cut accepted foods.

CHAPTER 3:

What You Can Eat

Depending on the type of diet plan that you choose, you have to eat a number of lean and green meals that are comprised mainly of lean proteins and non-starchy vegetables. Although this diet regimen is not as restrictive as other diet regimens, this means that there are plenty of foods that are compliant with this diet, including healthy fats. Thus, below are the types of foods that you can eat while following the Optavia diet.

Optavia fuelings: The Optavia Diet is famous for its Optavia fuelings that involve pre-packaged foods that dieters can eat. There are more than 60 soups, shakes, bars, and other fueling products that you can consume as your meal replacements.

Lean meats: Lean and green meals require you to make foods out of lean meats. There are three categories of lean meats identified by Optavia, including (1) lean, (2) leaner, and (3) leanest. Lean meats include salmon, pork chops, and lamb, while leaner meats include chicken breasts and swordfish. Leanest meats include egg whites, shrimp, and cod.

Green and non-starchy vegetables: Non-starchy vegetables are further identified as (1) lower carb, (2) moderate carb, and (3) higher carb. Lower carbs include all types of salad greens and green leafy vegetables. Moderate carb vegetables include summer squash and cauliflower. Lastly, high carb vegetables include peppers and broccoli.

Healthy fats: Healthy fats are encouraged for people who follow the Optavia Diet. These include healthy fats such as olive oil, walnut oil, flaxseed, and avocado. However, it is important to consume two servings of healthy fats to still keep up with the Optavia Diet.

Others: Once dieters are able to achieve their weight loss goals through meal replacements, they can start consuming other foods to maintain their ideal weight. These include low-fat dairy, fresh fruits, and whole grains. You can also consume meatless alternatives, including 2 cups egg substitute and 5 ounces seitan. For low-fat dairy, you are allowed to consume 1 ½ cups 1% cottage cheese and 12 ounces of non-fat Greek yogurt.

What Not to Eat

Similar to other diet regimens, the Optavia Diet also discourages dieters not to eat certain types of foods. This section will discuss the foods that are non-compliant with the principles of the Optavia Diet.

Indulgent desserts: This diet regimen discourages the consumption of indulgent desserts such as cakes, ice cream, cookies, and all kinds of pastries. While eating these foods is discouraged during the first few weeks of following the diet, moderate consumption of sweet treats such as fresh fruits and yogurts can be integrated into one's diet.

Sugary beverages: Similar to indulgent desserts, sugary beverages are also discouraged among those who follow the Optavia Diet. These include soda, fruit juices, and energy drinks.

Unhealthy fats: Fats such as butter, shortening, and commercial salad dressings contain large amounts of calories that are not good for people who are trying to lose weight. Moreover, they also contain preservatives and salt that is not good for the overall health.

Alcohol: Those who follow the Optavia Diet should limit their alcohol intake to 5 ounces of alcohol daily.

How Often Can You Eat?

The Optavia Diet plan teaches you the habit of eating healthy. You are encouraged to eat six small meals daily. As mentioned earlier, you are encouraged to eat every two to three hours from your waking time. Thus, start your day with Fuelings and eat your Lean and Green meals in between your Fuelings. It is recommended that you eat your first meal within an hour of waking to ensure optimal blood sugar. This is also a good strategy for hunger control.

The Optavia exhorts eating six or seven times each day (about each a few hours) contingents upon the arrangement. The three accessible plans are:

5&1 Plan: Consume 5 Optavia Fuelings & 1 "Lean and Green" supper per day.

4&2&1 Plan: Consume 4 Optavia Fuelings, 2 "Lean and Green" for dinner, and 1 snack per day.

3&3 Plan: Consume 3 Optavia Fuelings and 3 "Lean and Green" suppers per day.

CHAPTER 4:

The Differences Between Optavia Diet and Other Famous Diets

Linked to the Medifast plan, the Optavia Diet focuses primarily on mixes, snacks, and processed meals, with at least one low-carbohydrate meal—known as "Lean Green Meal"—that you cook on your own.

How Optavia differs from the initial Medifast plan is that you don't have to attend a doctor's clinic to sign up for or order items for the Optavia Diet. Getting started basically involves literally registering and paying electronically to get your first package delivered to you. And this facility, together with direct marketing and social networking, has undoubtedly played a significant role in making Optavia a common brand in the field of weight loss.

Thanks to the dynamic approach of Optavia, US World Report rated #2 on their Best Quick Weight-Loss Diets ranking. Apart from being at the top of the Best Diets chart, some amazing help and ease are given to customers to make their weight loss journey smoother.

It is easy to pick a plan and order, and automated fulfillment is possible. The most complicated directions for Optavia meals include the inclusion of water and microwaving. Food preparation is easy. It should be possible for even untrained cooks to easily tackle the lean and green dinner.

Optavia mentors seek to help you develop healthier practices, allowing you access to weekly and monthly calls to give support, group activities, and the wellness support network, which comprises experts such as licensed dietitians while becoming part of the Optavia network. A variety of detailed guides and FAQs can also be downloaded online for free.

Medifast also notes that its meals have a strong "fullness index," which indicates that the high quality of protein and fiber can leave you feeling satiated for longer. Experts on nutrition discuss the value of satiety, the relaxed sensation that you have had plenty.

The Different Phases

The Optavia Diet has two unique phases: Initial and Maintenance Phases. Upon enrollment, you will be assigned a diet coach that will help you undertake all the necessary things in order to be a successful dieter. So, if you are wondering what the steps that you need to undertake while following the two phases are, then this section will discuss just that.

The initial phase is when people are encouraged to limit their calorie intake from 800 to 1,000 calories for the next 12 weeks or until the dieter loses 12 pounds. For this phase, dieters are encouraged to consume lean and green meals five to seven times daily. Moreover, dieters are also encouraged to consume 1 optional snack, including sugar-free gelatin, celery sticks, and 12 ounces of nuts.

The maintenance phase, on the other hand, is implemented once you have already lost the 12 pounds from your initial weight. During this phase, you can increase your calorie intake to 1,550 dailies. This phase can last for 6 weeks. Moreover, you are also allowed to incorporate other foods such as whole grains, fruits, and low-fat dairy into your diet.

After the maintenance phase, you are not ready to follow your specific Optavia Diet plan. This is also the time when you need to consume not only lean and green meals but also fueling foods. The number of meals depends on the specific diet plan you choose.

CHAPTER 5:
Breakfast

Cheeses Waffles

Preparation time: 10 minutes
Cooking time: 20 minutes
Servings: 4
Ingredients:
- 1 large egg, beaten
- 1 cup ricotta cheese, crumbled
- ¼ cup low-fat Parmesan cheese, grated
- 4 oz. frozen spinach, thawed and squeezed dry
- 1 garlic clove, minced
- Salt and freshly ground black pepper, to taste

Directions:
1. Preheat a mini waffle iron and then grease it.
2. In a bowl, add all the ingredients and beat until well combined.
3. Place ¼ of the mixture into preheated waffle iron and cook for about 4–5 minutes or until golden brown.
4. Repeat with the remaining mixture.
5. Serve warm.

Nutrition: calories 140, fat 7, fiber 1, carbs 5, protein 12.

Super-Food Scramble

Preparation time: 10 minutes
Cooking time: 10 minutes
Servings: 2
Ingredients:
- 4 eggs
- 1/8 tsp. ground turmeric
- 1/8 tsp. red pepper flakes, crushed
- Salt and freshly ground black pepper, to taste
- 1 tbsp. water
- 2 tsp. olive oil
- 1 cup fresh kale, tough ribs removed and chopped

Directions:
1. In a bowl, add the eggs, turmeric, red pepper flakes, salt, black pepper, and water, and with a whisk, beat until foamy.
2. In a skillet, heat the oil over medium heat.

3. Add the egg mixture and stir to combine.
4. Immediately, reduce the heat to medium-low and cook for about 1–2 minutes, stirring frequently.
5. Stir in the kale and cook for about 3–4 minutes, stirring frequently.
6. Remove from the heat and serve immediately.

Nutrition: Calories 240, fat 7, fiber 4, carbs 12, protein 12.

Healthier Scramble

Preparation time: 10 minutes
Cooking time: 8 minutes
Servings: 4
Ingredients:

- 6 eggs
- 2 tbsp. unsweetened almond milk
- Salt and freshly ground black pepper, to taste
- 2 tbsp. olive oil
- 4 oz. smoked salmon, cut into bite-sized chunks
- 2 C. fresh arugula, chopped finely
- 4 scallions, chopped finely

Directions:
1. In a bowl, place the eggs, coconut milk, salt, and black pepper and beat well. Set aside.
2. In a non-stick skillet, heat the oil over medium heat.
3. Place the egg mixture evenly and cook for about 30 seconds without stirring.
4. Place the salmon kale and scallions on top of the egg mixture evenly.
5. Reduce heat to low and cook, covered for about 4–5 minutes or until omelet is done completely.
6. Uncover the skillet and cook for about 1 minute.
7. Carefully transfer the omelet onto a serving plate and serve

Nutrition: calories 210, fat 7, fiber 1, carbs 5.2, protein 15.

Fall Morning Omelet

Preparation time: 10 minutes
Cooking time: 9 minutes
Servings: 4
Ingredients:

- 2 tsp. olive oil, divided
- ½ of large green apple, cored and sliced thinly
- ¼ tsp. ground cinnamon
- 2 large eggs
- 1/8 tsp. vanilla extract
- Pinch of salt

Directions:

1. In a non-stick frying pan, heat 1 tsp. oil over medium-low heat.
2. Add apple slices and sprinkle with nutmeg and cinnamon.
3. Cook for about 4–5 minutes, turning once halfway through.
4. Meanwhile, in a bowl, add eggs, vanilla extract, and salt and beat until fluffy.
5. Add the remaining oil to the pan and let it heat completely.
6. Place the egg mixture over apple slices evenly and cook for about 3–4 minutes or until desired doneness.
7. Carefully, turn the pan over a serving plate and immediately fold the omelet.
8. Serve hot.

Nutrition: calories 250, fat 7, fiber 1, carbs 9, protein 13.

Perfect Savory Waffles
Preparation time: 10 minutes
Cooking time: 8 minutes
Servings: 2
Ingredients:

- 1/3 cup broccoli, chopped finely.
- ¼ cup low-fat Cheddar cheese, shredded.
- 1 egg.
- ½ tsp. garlic powder.
- ½ tsp. dried onion, minced.
- Salt and freshly ground black pepper, to taste.

Directions:
1. Preheat a mini waffle iron and then grease it.
2. In a medium bowl, place all ingredients and mix until well combined.
3. Place ½ of the mixture into preheated waffle iron and cook for about 3–4 minutes or until golden brown.
4. Repeat with the remaining mixture.
5. Serve warm.

Nutrition: calories 94, fat 7, fiber 4, carbs 12, protein 6.2

Chicken Zucchini Noodles
Preparation time: 10 minutes
Cooking time: 20 minutes
Servings: 2
Ingredients:

- 1 large zucchini, spiraled
- 1 chicken breast, skinless & boneless
- ½ tbsp. jalapeno, minced
- 2 garlic cloves, minced
- ½ tsp. ginger, minced
- ½ tbsp. fish sauce

- 2 tbsp. coconut cream
- ½ tbsp. honey
- ½ lime juice
- 1 tbsp. peanut butter
- 1 carrot, chopped
- 2 tbsp. cashews, chopped
- ¼ cup fresh cilantro, chopped
- 1 tbsp. olive oil

Directions:
1. Heat olive oil in a pan over medium-high heat.
2. Season chicken breast with pepper and salt. Once the oil is hot then, adds chicken breast into the pan and cook for 3–4 minutes per side or until cooked.
3. Remove chicken breast from pan. Shred chicken breast with a fork and set aside.
4. In a small bowl, mix together peanut butter, jalapeno, garlic, ginger, fish sauce, coconut cream, honey, and lime juice. Set aside.
5. In a large mixing bowl, combine together spiraled zucchini, carrots, cashews, cilantro, and shredded chicken.
6. Pour peanut butter mixture over zucchini noodles and toss to combine.
7. Serve immediately and enjoy it.

Nutrition: calories 353, fat 7, fiber 1, carbs 22, protein 25.

Eggless Scramble

Preparation time: 10 minutes
Cooking time: 9 minutes
Servings: 4
Ingredients:
- 1 tbsp. olive oil
- 1 garlic clove, minced
- ¼ lb. medium-firm tofu, drained, pressed, and crumbled
- 1/3 cup vegetable broth
- 2¾ cup fresh baby spinach
- 2 tsp. low-sodium soy sauce
- 1 tsp. ground turmeric
- 1 tsp. fresh lemon juice

Directions:
1. In a frying pan, heat the olive oil over medium-high heat and sauté the garlic for about 1 minute.
2. Add the tofu and cook for about 2–3 minutes, slowly adding the broth.
3. Add the spinach, soy sauce, and turmeric and stir fry for about 3–4 minutes or until all the liquid is absorbed.
4. Stir in the lemon juice and remove from the heat.
5. Serve immediately.

Nutrition: calories 130, fat 7, fiber 3, carbs 5.2, protein 9.

Parmesan Zucchini
Preparation time: 10 minutes
Cooking time: 30 minutes
Servings: 4
Ingredients:
- 4 zucchini, quartered lengthwise
- 2 tbsp. olive oil
- ¼ tsp. garlic powder
- ½ tsp. dried basil
- ½ tsp. dried oregano
- ½ tsp. dried thyme
- ½ cup parmesan cheese, grated

Directions:
1. Preheat the oven to 350° F. Line baking sheet with parchment paper and set aside.
2. In a small bowl, mix together parmesan cheese, garlic powder, basil, oregano, thyme, pepper, and salt.
3. Arrange zucchini onto the prepared baking sheet and drizzle with oil and sprinkle with parmesan cheese mixture.
4. Bake in preheated oven for 15 minutes, then broil for 2 minutes or until lightly golden brown.
5. Garnish with parsley and serve immediately.

Nutrition: calories 244, fat 17, fiber 4, carbs 7, protein 16.

Creamy Cauliflower Soup
Preparation time: 10 minutes
Cooking time: 30 minutes
Servings: 6
Ingredients:
- 5 cups cauliflower rice
- 8 oz. cheddar cheese, grated
- 2 cups unsweetened almond milk
- 2 cups vegetable stock
- 2 tbsp. water
- 1 small onion, chopped
- 2 garlic cloves, minced
- 1 tbsp. olive oil

Directions:
1. Heat olive oil in a large stockpot over medium heat.
2. Add onion and garlic and cook for 1–2 minutes.
3. Add cauliflower rice and water. Cover and cook for 5–7 minutes.
4. Now add vegetable stock and almond milk and stir well. Bring to boil.

5. Turn heat to low and simmer for 5 minutes.
6. Turn off the heat. Slowly add cheddar cheese and stir until smooth.
7. Season soup with pepper and salt.
8. Stir well and serve hot.

Nutrition: calories 240, fat 7, fiber 4, carbs 12, protein 12.

Taco Zucchini Boats

Preparation time: 10 minutes
Cooking time: 30 minutes
Servings: 4
Ingredients:

- 4 medium zucchinis cut in half lengthwise
- ¼ cup fresh cilantro, chopped
- ½ cup cheddar cheese, shredded
- ¼ cup water
- 4 oz. tomato sauce
- 2 tbsp. bell pepper, mined
- ½ small onion, minced
- ½ tsp. oregano
- 1 tsp. paprika
- 1 tsp. chili powder
- 1 tsp. cumin
- 1 tsp. garlic powder
- 1 lb. lean ground turkey
- ½ cup salsa
- 1 tsp. kosher salt

Directions:
1. Preheat the oven to 400° F.
2. Add ¼ cup of salsa to the bottom of the baking dish.
3. Using a spoon, hollow out the center of the zucchini halves.
4. Chop the scooped-out flesh of zucchini and set aside ¾ of a cup of chopped flesh.
5. Add zucchini halves to the boiling water and cook for 1 minute. Remove zucchini halves from water.
6. Add ground turkey in a large pan and cook until meat is no longer pink. Add spices and mix well.
7. Add reserved zucchini flesh, water, tomato sauce, bell pepper, and onion. Stir well and cover, simmer over low heat for 20 minutes.
8. Stuff zucchini boats with taco meat and top each with one tablespoon of shredded cheddar cheese.
9. Place zucchini boats in baking dish. Cover dish with foil and bake in preheated oven for 35 minutes.
10. Top with remaining salsa and chopped cilantro.

11. Serve and enjoy it.

Nutrition: calories 240, fat 7, fiber 4, carbs 12, protein 12.

Chinese Style Scramble

Preparation time: 10 minutes
Cooking time: 5 minutes
Servings: 4
Ingredients:

- 4 eggs
- ¼ tsp. red pepper flakes, crushed
- Salt and freshly ground black pepper, to taste
- ¼ cup fresh basil, chopped
- ½ cup tomatoes, chopped

Directions:
1. In a large bowl, add eggs, red pepper flakes, salt, and black pepper and beat well.
2. Add the basil and tomatoes and stir to combine.
3. In a large non-stick skillet, heat oil over medium-high heat.
4. Add the egg mixture and cook for about 3–5 minutes, stirring continuously.
5. Serve immediately.

Nutrition: calories 240, fat 7, fiber 4, carbs 12, protein 12.

Pesto Zucchini Noodles

Preparation time: 10 minutes
Cooking time: 30 minutes
Servings: 4
Ingredients:

- 1 tbsp. avocado oil
- 2 garlic cloves, chopped
- 1/3 cup parmesan cheese, grated
- 2 cups fresh basil
- 1/3 cup almonds
- 1/8 tsp. black pepper
- ¾ tsp. sea salt

Directions:
1. Add zucchini noodles into a colander and sprinkle with ¼ teaspoon of salt. Cover and let sit for 30 minutes. Drain zucchini noodles well and pat dry.
2. Preheat the oven to 400°F.
3. Place almonds on a parchment-lined baking sheet and bake for 6–8 minutes.
4. Transfer toasted almonds into the food processor and process until coarse.
5. Add olive oil, cheese, basil, garlic, pepper, and remaining salt in a food processor with almonds and process until pesto texture.
6. Heat avocado oil in a large pan over medium-high heat.

7. Add zucchini noodles and cook for 4–5 minutes.
8. Pour pesto over zucchini noodles, mix well and cook for 1 minute.
9. Serve immediately with baked salmon.

Nutrition: calories 540, fat 47, fiber 4, carbs 9.2, protein 17.

Baked Cod & Vegetables

Preparation time: 10 minutes
Cooking time: 30 minutes
Servings: 4
Ingredients:

- 1 lb. cod fillets
- 8 oz. asparagus, chopped
- 3 cups broccoli, chopped
- ¼ cup parsley, minced
- ½ tsp. lemon pepper seasoning
- ½ tsp. paprika
- ¼ cup olive oil
- ¼ cup lemon juice
- 1 tsp. salt

Directions:
1. Preheat the oven to 400°F. Line baking sheet with parchment paper and set aside.
2. In a small bowl, mix together lemon juice, paprika, olive oil, lemon pepper seasoning, and salt.
3. Place fish fillets in the middle of the parchment paper. Place broccoli and asparagus around the fish fillets.
4. Pour lemon juice mixture over the fish fillets and top with parsley.
5. Bake in preheated oven for 13–15 minutes.
6. Serve and enjoy it.

Nutrition: calories 240, fat 17, fiber 4, carbs 7, protein 22.

Healthy Broccoli Salad

Preparation time: 10 minutes
Cooking time: 10 minutes
Servings: 4
Ingredients:

- 3 cups broccoli, chopped
- 1 tbsp. apple cider vinegar
- ½ cup Greek yogurt
- 3 bacon slices, cooked and chopped
- 1/3 cup onion, sliced
- ¼ tsp. stevia

Directions:

1. In a mixing bowl, mix together broccoli, onion, and bacon.
2. In a small bowl, mix together yogurt, vinegar, and stevia and pour over broccoli mixture. Stir to combine.
3. Sprinkle sunflower seeds on top of the salad.
4. Store salad in the refrigerator for 30 minutes.
5. Serve and enjoy it.

Nutrition: calories 90, fat 7, fiber 4, carbs 5.2, protein 6.

Tomato Cucumber Avocado Salad

Preparation time: 10 minutes
Cooking time: 15 Minutes
Servings: 4
Ingredients:

- 12 oz. cherry tomatoes cut in half
- 5 small cucumbers, chopped
- 3 small avocados, chopped
- ½ tsp. ground black pepper
- 2 tbsp. olive oil
- 2 tbsp. fresh lemon juice
- ¼ cup fresh cilantro, chopped
- 1 tsp. sea salt

Directions:

1. Add cherry tomatoes, cucumbers, avocados, and cilantro into the large mixing bowl and mix well.
2. Mix together olive oil, lemon juice, black pepper, and salt and pour over salad.
3. Toss well and serve immediately.

Nutrition: calories 440, fat 7, fiber 4, carbs 12, protein 6.

CHAPTER 6:
Poultry

Caesar Chicken Lettuce Wraps
Preparation time: 10 minutes
Cooking time: 30 minutes
Servings: 4
Ingredients:

- Raw - boneless - skinless chicken breasts (24 oz. - leaner-leans)
- Walden Farms Caesar Salad Dressing (2 tbsp. - condiment)
- Black pepper (0.5 tsp. - condiment)
- Salt (0.5 tsp. - condiment)
- Oregano (0.25 tsp. - condiment)
- Olive oil (1 tbsp. - healthy fats)
- Romaine lettuce (8 to 12 leaves - greens)
- Grated reduced-fat parmesan cheese (2 tbsp. - condiment)

Directions:
1. Slice the chicken into strips and sauté in olive oil until done.
2. Toss the rest of the fixings (omit the lettuce) with the chicken in a food processor to chop. Pulse it about six or eight times, but do not finely chop it.
3. After it's processed, you need to weigh and use only six ounces of the prepared chicken to fill the lettuce leaves. Lightly dust each wrap with parmesan and serve.

Nutrition: calories 240, fat 7, fiber 4, carbs 12, protein 12.

Chicken Fillets with Artichoke Hearts
Preparation time: 10 minutes
Cooking time: 30 minutes
Servings: 3
Ingredients:

- 1 Can artichoke hearts, chopped
- 12 oz. chicken fillets (3 oz. each fillet)
- 1 teaspoon avocado oil
- ½ teaspoon ground thyme
- ½ teaspoon white pepper
- 1/3 cup of water
- 1/3 cup shallot, roughly chopped
- 1 lemon, sliced

Directions:

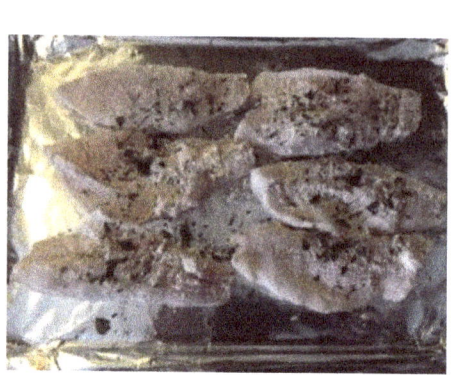

1. Mix up together chicken fillets, artichoke hearts, avocado oil, ground thyme, white pepper, and shallot.
2. Line the baking tray with baking paper and place the chicken fillet mixture in it.
3. Then add sliced lemon and water.
4. Bake the meal for 30 minutes at 375°F. Stir the ingredients during cooking to avoid burning.

Nutrition: Calories 267, Fat 8.2, Fiber 3.8, Carbs 10.4 g, Protein 35.2

Almond-Maple Chicken

Preparation time: 10 minutes
Cooking time: 30 minutes
Servings: 4
Ingredients:

- Chicken breasts (8 oz. raw/yield 6 oz. cooked - leaner lean)
- Walden Farms pancake syrup (2 tbsp. - condiment)
- Fresh lemon zest (0.5 tbsp. - condiment)
- Lemon juice (1 tsp. - condiment)
- Salt (0.25 tsp. - condiment)
- Pepper (1/8 tsp. - condiment)
- Almonds (10 whole - optional snacks)

Directions:
1. Warm the oven to reach 400°F. Grate the lemon rind and chop the almonds.
2. Arrange the chicken in a shallow baking pan and dust with pepper and salt.
3. Whisk and combine the rind of the lemon, pancake syrup, almonds, and lemon juice in a mixing container.
4. Pour it over the chicken and bake until it's done (25–30 min.) before serving.

Nutrition: calories 240, fat 7, fiber 4, carbs 12, protein 12.

Chicken Loaf

Preparation time: 10 minutes
Cooking time: 40 minutes
Servings: 4
Ingredients:

- 2 cups ground chicken
- 1 egg, beaten
- 1 tablespoon fresh dill, chopped
- 1 garlic clove, chopped
- ½ teaspoon salt
- 1 teaspoon chili flakes
- 1 onion, minced

Directions:
1. In the mixing bowl, combine together all ingredients and mix up until you get a smooth mass.

2. Then line the loaf dish with baking paper and put the ground chicken mixture inside.
3. Flatten the surface well.
4. Bake the chicken loaf for 40 minutes at 355°F.
5. Then chill the chicken loaf to room temperature and remove from the loaf dish.
6. Slice it.

Nutrition: Calories 167, Fat 6.2, Fiber 0.8, Carbs 3.4, Protein 32.

Buffalo Chicken Spaghetti Squash
Preparation time: 10 minutes
Cooking time: 30 minutes
Servings: 1
Ingredients:

- Cooked spaghetti squash (1 cup - greens)
- Cabbage/coleslaw mix (0.5 cup - green)
- Garlic powder (0.25 tsp. - condiment)
- Onion powder (1/8 tsp. - condiment)
- Cooked chicken breasts (4.5 oz. - leaner)
- Frank's buffalo hot sauce (2 tbsp. - condiment)
- Shredded reduced-fat mozzarella cheese (0.25 cup - lean)
- Light ranch dressing (1.5 tbsp. - healthy fat)

Directions:
1. Chop the cabbage or purchase a tri-color coleslaw mix and discard the carrots. Chop the baked or grilled chicken into pieces.
2. Prepare a skillet using the med-high temperature setting. Add the cabbage and spaghetti squash.
3. Mix in the hot sauce, garlic powder, onion powder, and chicken. Simmer gently until it's thoroughly heated and combined.
4. Sprinkle with shredded mozzarella cheese and let it melt.
5. Drizzle a portion of ranch dressing over the top before serving.

Nutrition: calories 240, fat 7, fiber 4, carbs 12, protein 14.

Chicken Alfredo
Preparation time: 10 minutes
Cooking time: 30 minutes
Servings: 1
Ingredients:

- Grilled/baked chicken - sliced/diced (4 oz. - leaner)

The Alternative Pasta:
- Spiraled yellow squash/zucchini or both (1.5 cups - greens)
- Olive oil (1 tsp. - healthy fat)
- Dried basil (0.25 tsp. - condiment)

The Sauce:

- 1% cottage cheese (0.5 cup - leaner)
- Salt (1/8 tsp. - condiment)
- Garlic powder (0.5 tsp. - condiment)
- Parmesan cheese - grated & reduced-fat (1 tbsp. - condiment)
- Almond milk - unsweetened (1 tbsp. - condiment)
- Freshly cracked black pepper (1/8 tsp. - condiment)

Directions:
1. You can choose to leave the peel on the squash for more color and extra fiber or remove it for a noodle similarity. Discard both ends and measure out 1 ½ cups of the finished product.
2. Add one teaspoon of oil to a skillet and warm it using the medium-high temperature setting. Toss in the spiraled squash and cook until the squash is tender (2 min.). Add the basil, salt, pepper, or garlic powder as desired. Set it aside in a container for now.
3. Make the sauce by combining the cottage cheese with the garlic powder, salt, almond milk, pepper, and parmesan cheese, and pepper in a blender until the mixture is smooth.
4. Add the sauce into a microwave-safe dish and heat until warm (about 45 seconds to 1 minute), checking at 15-second intervals to stir.
5. Arrange the chicken over the tasty pasta and serve with a portion of the sauce over the top.

Nutrition: calories 240, fat 7, fiber 4, carbs 12, protein 12.

Broccoli Chicken Dijon
Preparation time: 10 minutes
Cooking time: 30 minutes
Servings: 4
Ingredients:

- Chicken breasts - cut into strips (18 oz. - should yield 12 oz. cooked - leaner leans)
- Reduced-sodium chicken broth (0.25 cup - condiment)
- Light soy sauce (1 tbsp. - condiment)
- Olive oil (2 tsp. - healthy fat)
- Broccoli florets (3 cups - greens)
- Garlic (1 clove - condiment)
- Dijon mustard (1 tbsp. - condiment)

Directions:
1. Either purchase the chicken pre-sliced or remove the skin and bones before you begin.
2. In a bowl, coat the chicken in a mixing container using soy sauce and marinate for half an hour for enhanced flavor.
3. Mince and sauté the garlic, broccoli, and one teaspoon olive oil using the medium-temperature setting until lightly browned. Transfer the skillet from the burner and set it aside (covered) so it will remain warm.
4. Pour the rest of the oil into a skillet and stir-fry the chicken for four to seven minutes or until cooked thoroughly. Pour in the chicken broth and mustard.

5. Once heated, adjust the temperature setting to med-low, and stir the broccoli mixture into the skillet. Mix until heated thoroughly, stirring occasionally.
6. Portion the chicken and serve.

Nutrition: calories 240, fat 7, fiber 4, carbs 12, protein 12.

Turkey Burgers

Preparation time: 10 minutes
Cooking time: 30 minutes
Servings: 4
Ingredients:

- 1 lb. lean ground turkey
- 2 green onions, sliced
- ¼ cup basil leaves, shredded
- 2 garlic cloves, minced
- 2 medium zucchini shredded and squeeze out all the liquid
- ½ tsp. black pepper
- ½ tsp. sea salt

Directions:
1. Heat grill to medium heat.
2. Add all ingredients into the mixing bowl and mix until well combined.
3. Make four equal shapes of patties from the mixture.
4. Spray one piece of foil with cooking spray.
5. Place prepared patties on the foil and grill for 10 minutes. Turn patties to the other side and grill for 10 minutes more.

Nutrition: calories 140, fat 7, fiber 4, carbs 12, protein 8.

Grilled Marinated Chicken

Preparation time: 35 minutes
Cooking time: 20 minutes
Servings: 6
Ingredients:

- 2-pound chicken breast, skinless, boneless
- 2 tablespoons lemon juice
- 1 teaspoon sage
- ½ teaspoon ground nutmeg
- ½ teaspoon dried oregano
- 1 teaspoon paprika
- 1 teaspoon onion powder
- 2 tablespoons olive oil
- 1 teaspoon chili flakes
- 1 teaspoon salt
- 1 teaspoon apple cider vinegar

Directions:
1. Make the marinade: whisk together apple cider vinegar, salt, chili flakes, olive oil, onion powder, paprika, dried oregano, ground nutmeg, sage, and lemon juice.
2. Then rub the chicken with marinade carefully and leave for 25 minutes to marinate.
3. Meanwhile, preheat grill to 385°F.
4. Place the marinated chicken breast in the grill and cook it for 10 minutes from each side.
5. Cut the cooked chicken on the servings.

Nutrition: Calories 218Fat 8.2, Fiber 0.8, Carbs 0.4, Protein 32.2

Chicken Casserole

Preparation time: 10 minutes
Cooking time: 40 minutes
Servings: 4
Ingredients:
- 1 lb. cooked chicken, shredded
- ¼ cup Greek yogurt
- 1 cup cheddar cheese, shredded
- ½ cup of salsa
- 4 oz. cream cheese, softened
- 4 cups cauliflower florets
- 1/8 tsp. black pepper
- ½ tsp. kosher salt

Directions:
1. Add cauliflower florets into the microwave-safe dish and cook for 10 minutes or until tender.
2. Add cream cheese and microwave for 30 seconds more. Stir well.
3. Add chicken, yogurt, cheddar cheese, salsa, pepper, and salt, and stir everything well.
4. Preheat the oven to 375° F.
5. Bake in preheated oven for 20 minutes.
6. Serve hot and enjoy it.

Nutrition: calories 240, fat 7, fiber 4, carbs 12, protein 12.

Chicken Saute

Preparation time: 10 minutes
Cooking time: 25 minutes
Servings: 2
Ingredients:
- 4 oz. chicken fillet
- 4 tomatoes, peeled
- 1 bell pepper, chopped
- 1 teaspoon olive oil
- 1 cup of water

- 1 teaspoon salt
- 1 chili pepper, chopped
- ½ teaspoon saffron

Directions:
1. Pour water into the pan and bring it to boil.
2. Meanwhile, chop the chicken fillet.
3. Add the chicken fillet to the boiling water and cook it for 10 minutes or until the chicken is tender.
4. After this, put the chopped bell pepper and chili pepper in the skillet.
5. Add olive oil and roast the vegetables for 3 minutes.
6. Add chopped tomatoes and mix up well.
7. Cook the vegetables for 2 minutes more.
8. Then add salt and a ¾ cup of water from chicken.
9. Add chopped chicken fillet and mix up.
10. Cook the sauté for 10 minutes over medium heat.

Nutrition: Calories 192, Fat 7.2 g, Fiber 3.8 g, Carbs 14.4 g, Protein 19.2 g

CHAPTER 7:
Seafood

Blackened Shrimps with Salad Lettuce

Preparation time: 10 minutes
Cooking time: 6 minutes
Servings: 4
Ingredients:
- 2 pounds raw shrimps peeled and deveined
- 1 tablespoon old bay blackened seasoning
- 4 teaspoons olive oil, divided
- 1 cup plain 2% Greek yogurt
- 6 ounces avocado
- 2 tablespoons lime juice, divided
- 1 ½ cups diced tomatoes
- ¼ cup diced green bell pepper
- ¼ cup chopped red onion
- 1 chopped jalapeno pepper
- 12 large romaine lettuces, torn

Directions:
1. Season the shrimps with the Old Bay seasoning and place in a plastic bag to marinate in the fridge for 1 hour.
2. Heat two teaspoons of olive oil in a skillet and add the shrimps. Cook for 3 minutes until the shrimps are slightly pink. Set aside.
3. Combine the yogurt and avocado. Season with lime juice and pulse in a blender until smooth.
4. In a bowl, combine the rest of the ingredients and add the shrimp. Spread over the sauce.
5. Toss to coat.

Nutrition: calories 390, fat 7, fiber 3, carbs 10, protein 50.

Shrimp Cobb Salad

Preparation time: 10 minutes
Cooking time: 10 minutes
Servings: 1
Ingredients:
- 2 cups romaine lettuce, cleaned and torn
- 4 ounces cooked and peeled shrimps
- ½ cup cherry tomatoes, halved
- 1 hard-boiled egg, sliced
- 1/8 avocado, diced

- 1 tablespoon ranch dressing

Directions:
1. Place all ingredients in a bowl and toss to combine everything.
2. Serve immediately.

Nutrition: calories 340, fat 7, fiber 4, carbs 12, protein 32.

Broccoli Kale Salmon Burgers

Preparation time: 10 minutes
Cooking time: 30 minutes
Servings: 5
Ingredients:
- 2 eggs
- ½ cup onion, chopped
- ½ cup broccoli, chopped
- ½ cup kale, chopped
- ½ tsp. garlic powder
- 2 tbsp. lemon juice
- ½ cup almond flour
- 15 oz. can salmon, drained and bones removed
- ½ tsp. salt

Directions:
1. Line one plate with parchment paper and set aside.
2. Add all ingredients into the large bowl and mix until well combined.
3. Make five equal shapes of patties from the mixture and place them on a prepared plate.
4. Place plate in the refrigerator for 30 minutes.
5. Spray a large pan with cooking spray and heat over medium heat.
6. Once the pan is hot, then add patties and cook for 5–7 minutes per side.
7. Serve and enjoy it.

Nutrition: calories 240, fat 7, fiber 4, carbs 12, protein 12.

Lemon-Garlic Scallops

Preparation time: 10 minutes
Cooking time: 15 minutes
Servings: 1
Ingredients:
- 7 ounces scallops
- 1 teaspoon olive oil
- ½ teaspoon garlic powder
- 1 tablespoon lemon juice

Directions:

1. Preheat the oven to 400°F.
2. Place all ingredients in a Ziploc bag and allow marinating in the fridge for 1 hour.
3. Place the scallops on a foil-lined baking sheet.
4. Bake in the oven for 15 minutes.

Nutrition: calories 185, fat 6, fiber 4, carbs 8, protein 24.

Shrimp Cucumber Salad

Preparation time: 10 minutes
Cooking time: 30 minutes
Servings: 4
Ingredients:

- 1 lb. shrimp, cooked
- 1 bell pepper, sliced
- 2 green onions, sliced
- ½ cup fresh cilantro, chopped
- 2 cucumbers, sliced

For Dressing:

- 2 tbsp. fresh mint leaves, chopped
- 1 tsp. sesame seeds
- ½ tsp. red pepper flakes
- 1 tbsp. olive oil
- ¼ cup rice wine vinegar
- ¼ cup lime juice
- 1 Serrano chili pepper, minced
- 3 garlic cloves, minced
- ½ tsp. salt

Directions:

1. In a small bowl, whisk together all dressing ingredients and set aside.
2. In a mixing bowl, mix together shrimp, bell pepper, green onion, cilantro, and cucumbers.
3. Pour dressing over salad and toss well.
4. Serve and enjoy it.

Nutrition: calories 120, fat 7, fiber 4, carbs 12, protein 2.

Steamed White Fish Tacos

Preparation time: 10 minutes
Cooking time: 15 minutes
Servings: 2
Ingredients:

- 1-pound raw cod filets
- ½ teaspoon garlic powder
- ½ teaspoon salt, divided

- ½ cup diced tomato
- 2 tablespoons chopped red onion
- ½ jalapeno pepper, chopped
- 2 tablespoons chopped fresh cilantro
- 1 tablespoon lime juice
- 6 ounces avocado, sliced, and meat scooped out
- 6 large romaine lettuce leaves

Directions:
1. Season the cod with garlic powder and salt. Steam the fish for 10 minutes. Flake the fish using a fork and remove any bones. Set aside to cool.
2. In a bowl, combine the tomatoes, onions, jalapeno pepper, cilantro, and lime juice.
3. Assemble the tacos.
4. Layer the fish, tomato mixture, and avocado on top of the lettuce leaves.
5. Serve immediately.

Nutrition: calories 426, fat 7, fiber 4, carbs 72, protein 32.

Asparagus & Shrimp Stir Fry

Preparation time: 10 minutes
Cooking time: 20 minutes
Servings: 4
Ingredients:
- 1 lb. asparagus
- 1 lb. shrimp
- 2 tbsp. lemon juice
- 1 tbsp. soy sauce
- 1 tps. ginger minced
- 1 garlic clove, minced
- 1 tsp. red pepper flakes
- ¼ cup olive oil

Directions:
1. Heat 2 tablespoons of oil in a large pan over medium-high heat.
2. Add shrimp to the pan and season with red pepper flakes, pepper, and salt, and cook for 5 minutes.
3. Remove shrimp from pan and set aside.
4. Add remaining oil in the same pan. Add garlic, ginger, and asparagus and stir frequently and cook until asparagus is tender about 5 minutes.
5. Return shrimp to the pan. Add lemon juice and soy sauce and stir until well combined.
6. Serve hot and enjoy it.

Nutrition: calories 240, fat 7, fiber 4, carbs 12, protein 9.

Shrimp Scampi

Preparation time: 10 minutes
Cooking time: 25 minutes
Servings: 4
Ingredients:

- 1 small spaghetti squash cut in half and seeds removed
- 2 ½ tablespoons olive oil
- 1 clove of garlic, minced
- 1 ¾ pound peeled and deveined shrimps
- 1 cup cherry tomatoes, halved
- ½ teaspoon crushed red pepper flakes
- 1 teaspoon lemon juice
- 1 tablespoon dried parsley
- ½ teaspoon onion powder
- Salt and pepper to taste
- ¼ cup shredded Parmesan cheese

Directions:

1. Place the spaghetti squash in a steamer and steam for 20 minutes until tender. Allow to cool and scoop the flesh using a fork. Set aside.
2. Heat oil in a skillet over medium flame and sauté the garlic for 30 seconds or until fragrant. Stir in the shrimps and stir for 1 minute. Add in the tomatoes, pepper flakes, lemon juice, dried parsley, onion powder, and salt and pepper to taste. Stir for 3 minutes.
3. Pour the shrimps on top of the cooked spaghetti squash.
4. Garnish with parmesan cheese.

Nutrition: calories 340, fat 7, fiber 4, carbs 12, protein 43.

CHAPTER 8:
Vegetables

Taco Zucchini Boats

Preparation time: 10 minutes
Cooking time: 30 minutes
Servings: 4
Ingredients:

- 4 medium zucchinis cut in half lengthwise
- ¼ cup fresh cilantro, chopped
- ½ cup cheddar cheese, shredded
- ¼ cup of water
- 4 oz. tomato sauce
- 2 tbsp. bell pepper, mined
- ½ small onion, minced
- ½ tsp. oregano
- 1 tsp. paprika
- 1 tsp. chili powder
- 1 tsp. cumin
- 1 tsp. garlic powder
- 1 lb. lean ground turkey
- ½ cup of salsa
- 1 tsp. kosher salt

Directions:
1. Preheat the oven to 400° F.
2. Add ¼ cup of salsa to the bottom of the baking dish.
3. Using a spoon, hollow out the center of the zucchini halves.
4. Chop the scooped-out flesh of zucchini and set aside ¾ of a cup of chopped flesh.
5. Add zucchini halves to the boiling water and cook for 1 minute. Remove zucchini halves from water.
6. Add ground turkey in a large pan and cook until meat is no longer pink. Add spices and mix well.
7. Add reserved zucchini flesh, water, tomato sauce, bell pepper, and onion. Stir well and cover, simmer over low heat for 20 minutes.
8. Stuff zucchini boats with taco meat and top each with one tablespoon of shredded cheddar cheese.
9. Place zucchini boats in baking dish. Cover dish with foil and bake in preheated oven for 35 minutes.
10. Top with remaining salsa and chopped cilantro.

11. Serve and enjoy it.

Nutrition: calories 90, fat 8, fiber 4, carbs 6.2, protein 2.

Summer Vegetables

Preparation time: 20 minutes
Cooking time: 1 hour 40 minutes
Servings: 6
Ingredients:

- 1 teaspoon dried marjoram
- 1/3 cup Parmesan cheese
- 1 small eggplant, sliced into ¼-inch thick circles
- 1 small summer squash, peeled and sliced diagonally a ¼-inch thickness
- 3 large tomatoes, sliced into ¼-inch thick circles
- ½ cup dry white wine
- ½ teaspoon freshly ground pepper, divided
- ½ teaspoon salt, divided
- 5 cloves garlic, sliced thinly
- 2 cups leeks, sliced thinly
- 4 tablespoon extra-virgin olive oil, divided

Directions:
1. On medium fire, place a large non-stick saucepan and heat 2 tablespoon oil.
2. Sauté garlic and leeks for 6 minutes or until garlic is starting to brown. Season with pepper and salt, ¼ teaspoon each.
3. Pour in the wine and cook for another minute. Transfer to a 2-quart baking dish.
4. In a baking dish, layer in an alternating pattern the eggplant, summer squash, and tomatoes. Do this until the dish is covered with vegetables. If there are excess vegetables, store for future use.
5. Season with remaining pepper and salt. Drizzle with remaining olive oil and pop in a preheated 425°F oven.
6. Bake for 75 minutes. Remove from oven and top with marjoram and cheese.
7. Return to oven and bake for 15 minutes more or until veggies are soft and edges are browned.
8. Allow to cool for at least 5 minutes before serving.

Nutrition: calories 140, fat 7, fiber 4, carbs 12, protein 4.

Slow-Cooked Buttery Mushrooms

Preparation time: 10 minutes
Cooking time: 10 minutes
Servings: 2
Ingredients:

- 2 tablespoons butter

- 2 tablespoons olive oil
- 3 cloves of garlic, minced
- 16 ounces fresh brown mushrooms, sliced
- 7 ounces fresh shiitake mushrooms, sliced
- A dash of thyme
- Salt and pepper to taste

Directions:
1. Heat the butter and oil in a pot.
2. Sauté the garlic until fragrant, around 1 minute.
3. Stir in the rest of the ingredients and cook until soft, around 9 minutes.

Nutrition: Calories: 192; Carbs: 12.7; Protein: 3.8; Fat: 15.5

Pan-Seared Cod
Preparation time: 10 minutes
Cooking time: 20 minutes
Servings: 4
Ingredients:
- 1 ¾ lbs. cod fillets
- 1 tbsp. ranch seasoning
- 4 tsp. olive oil

Directions:
1. Heat oil in a large pan over medium-high heat.
2. Season fish fillets with ranch seasoning.
3. Once the oil is hot, then place fish fillets in a pan and cook for 6–8 minutes on each side.
4. Serve immediately and enjoy it.

Nutrition: calories 240, fat 7, fiber 4, carbs 12, protein 12.

Stir-Fried Brussels Sprouts and Carrots
Preparation time: 10 minutes
Cooking time: 15 minutes
Servings: 6
Ingredients:
- 1 tablespoon cider vinegar
- 1/3 cup water
- 1 lb. Brussels sprouts, halved lengthwise
- 1 lb. carrots cut diagonally into ½-inch thick lengths
- 3 tablespoon unsalted butter, divided
- 2 tablespoon chopped shallot
- ½ teaspoon pepper
- ¾ teaspoon salt

Directions:
1. On medium-high fire, place a non-stick medium fry pan and heat 2 tablespoon butter.
2. Add shallots and cook until softened, around one to two minutes while occasionally stirring.
3. Add pepper salt, Brussels sprouts, and carrots. Stir fry until vegetables start to brown on the edges, around 3 to 4 minutes.
4. Add water, cook, and cover.
5. After 5 to 8 minutes, or when veggies are already soft, add remaining butter.
6. If needed, season with more pepper and salt to taste.
7. Turn off fire, transfer to a platter, serve, and enjoy it.

Nutrition: Calories: 98; Carbs: 13.9g; Protein: 3.5g; Fat: 4.2g

Falafel Bites

Preparation time: 10 minutes
Cooking time: 15 minutes
Servings: 4
Ingredients:
- 1⅔ cups falafel mix
- 1¼ cups water
- Extra-virgin olive oil spray
- 1 tablespoon pickled onions
- 1 tablespoon pickled turnips
- 2 tablespoons Tzatziki Sauce (optional)

Direction:
1. In a large bowl, carefully stir the falafel mix into the water. Mix well. Let stand 15 minutes to absorb the water. Form mix into 1-inch balls and arrange on a baking sheet.
2. Preheat the broiler to high.
3. Take the balls and flatten slightly with your thumb (so they won't roll around on the baking sheet). Spray with olive oil and then broil for 2 to 3 minutes on each side until crispy and brown.
4. To fry the falafel, fill a pot with ½ inch of cooking oil and heat over medium-high heat to 375°F. Fry the balls for about 3 minutes, until brown and crisp. Drain on paper towels and serve with pickled onions, pickled turnips, and tzatziki sauce (if using).

Nutrition: Calories: 530; Carbs: 95.4g; Protein: 8.0g; Fat: 18.5g

Quick Lemon Pepper Salmon

Preparation time: 10 minutes
Cooking time: 19 minutes
Servings: 4
Ingredients:
- 1 ½ lbs. salmon fillet
- ½ tsp. ground black pepper
- 1 tsp. dried oregano
- 2 garlic cloves, minced

- ¼ cup olive oil
- 1 lemon juice
- 1 tsp. sea salt

Directions:
1. In a large bowl, mix together lemon juice, olive oil, garlic, oregano, black pepper, and salt.
2. Add fish fillets in bowl and coat well with marinade, and place in the refrigerator for 15 minutes.
3. Preheat the grill.
4. Brush grill grates with oil.
5. Place marinated salmon fillets on hot grill and cook for 4 minutes, then turn salmon fillets to the other side and cook for 4 minutes more.
6. Serve and enjoy it.

Nutrition: calories 240, fat 7, fiber 4, carbs 12, protein 12.

Steamed Zucchini-Paprika
Preparation time: 15 minutes
Cooking time: 30 minutes
Servings: 2
Ingredients:
- 4 tablespoons olive oil
- 3 cloves of garlic, minced
- 1 onion, chopped
- 3 medium-sized zucchinis, sliced thinly
- A dash of paprika
- Salt and pepper to taste

Directions:
1. Place all ingredients in the Instant Pot.
2. Give a good stir to combine all ingredients.
3. Close the lid and make sure that the steam release valve is set to "Venting."
4. Press the "Slow Cook" button and adjust the cooking time to 4 hours.
5. Halfway through the cooking time, open the lid and give a good stir to brown the other side.

Nutrition: Calories: 93; Carbs: 3.1g; Protein: 0.6g; Fat: 10.2

Delicious Zucchini Quiche
Preparation time: 10 minutes
Cooking time: 60 minutes
Servings: 8
Ingredients:
- 6 eggs
- 2 medium zucchini, shredded
- ½ tsp. dried basil
- 2 garlic cloves, minced

- 1 tbsp. dry onion, minced
- 2 tbsp. parmesan cheese, grated
- 2 tbsp. fresh parsley, chopped
- ½ cup olive oil
- 1 cup cheddar cheese, shredded
- ¼ cup coconut flour
- ¾ cup almond flour
- ½ tsp. salt

Directions:
1. Preheat the oven to 350°F. Grease 9-inch pie dish and set aside.
2. Squeeze out excess liquid from zucchini.
3. Add all ingredients into the large bowl and mix until well combined. Pour into the prepared pie dish.
4. Bake in preheated oven for 45–60 minutes or until set.
5. Remove from the oven and let it cool completely.
6. Slice and serve.

Nutrition: calories 240, fat 7, fiber 4, carbs 12, protein 12.

Stir-Fried Eggplant

Preparation time: 10 minutes
Cooking time: 30 minutes
Servings: 2
Ingredients:

- 1 teaspoon cornstarch + 2 tablespoon water, mixed
- 1 teaspoon brown sugar
- 2 tablespoon oyster sauce
- 1 tablespoon fish sauce
- 2 tablespoon soy sauce
- ½ cup fresh basil
- 2 tablespoon oil
- ¼ cup of water
- 2 cups Chinese eggplant, spiral
- 1 red chili
- 6 cloves garlic, minced
- ½ purple onion, sliced thinly
- 1 3-oz package medium-firm tofu, cut into slivers

Directions:
1. Prepare the sauce by mixing cornstarch and water in a small bowl. In another bowl, mix brown sugar, oyster sauce, and fish sauce and set aside.
2. On medium-high fire, place a large non-stick saucepan and heat 2 tablespoon oil. Sauté chili, garlic, and onion for 4 minutes. Add tofu, stir fry for 4 minutes.

3. Add eggplant noodles and stir fry for 10 minutes. If the pan dries up, add water in small amounts to moisten the pan and cook noodles.

4. Pour in the sauce and mix well. Once simmering, slowly add cornstarch mixer while continuing to mix vigorously. Once the sauce thickens, add fresh basil and cook for a minute.

5. Remove from fire, transfer to a serving plate, and enjoy it.

Nutrition: Calories: 369; Carbs: 28.4g; Protein: 11.4g; Fat: 25.3g

Tomato Avocado Salad

Preparation time: 10 minutes
Cooking time: 30 minutes
Servings: 4
Ingredients:

- 12 oz. cherry tomatoes cut in half
- 5 small cucumbers, chopped
- 3 small avocados, chopped
- ½ tsp. ground black pepper
- 2 tbsp. olive oil
- 2 tbsp. fresh lemon juice
- ¼ cup fresh cilantro, chopped
- 1 tsp. sea salt

Directions:

1. Add cherry tomatoes, cucumbers, avocados, and cilantro into the large mixing bowl and mix well.
2. Mix together olive oil, lemon juice, black pepper, and salt and pour over salad.
3. Toss well and serve immediately.

Nutrition: calories 440, fat 7, fiber 4, carbs 12, protein 7.

Tortellini in Red Pepper Sauce

Preparation time: 15 minutes
Cooking time: 10 minutes
Servings: 4
Ingredients:

- 1 (16-ounce) container fresh cheese tortellini (usually green and white pasta)
- 1 (16-ounce) jar roasted red peppers, drained
- 1 teaspoon garlic powder
- ¼ cup tahini
- 1 tablespoon red pepper oil (optional)

Directions:

1. Bring a large pot of water to a boil and cook the tortellini according to package directions.

2. In a blender, combine the red peppers with the garlic powder and process until smooth. Once blended, add the tahini until the sauce is thickened. If the sauce gets too thick, add up to 1 tablespoon red pepper oil (if using).

3. Once tortellini is cooked, drain and leave the pasta in a colander. Add the sauce to the bottom of the empty pot and heat for 2 minutes. Then, add the tortellini back into the pot and cook for 2 more minutes. Serve and enjoy it!

Nutrition: Calories: 530; Carbs: 95.4g; Protein: 8.0g; Fat: 18.5g

Quick Vegetable Kebabs

Preparation time: 15 minutes
Cooking time: 20 minutes
Servings: 6
Ingredients:
- 4 medium red onions peeled and sliced into 6 wedges
- 4 medium zucchini, cut into 1-inch-thick slices
- 4 bell peppers cut into 2-inch squares
- 2 yellow bell peppers cut into 2-inch squares
- 2 orange bell peppers cut into 2-inch squares
- 2 beefsteak tomatoes cut into quarters
- 3 tablespoons herbed oil

Direction:
1. Preheat the oven or grill to medium-high or 350°F.
2. Thread 1 piece of red onion, zucchini, different colored bell peppers, and tomatoes onto a skewer. Repeat until the skewer is full of vegetables, up to 2 inches away from the skewer end, and continue until all skewers are complete.
3. Put the skewers on a baking sheet and cook in the oven for 10 minutes or grill for 5 minutes on each side. The vegetables will be done with they reach your desired crunch or softness.
4. Remove the skewers from heat and drizzle with Herbed Oil.

Nutrition: Calories: 235; Carbs: 30.4g; Protein: 8.0g; Fat: 14.5g

Turkey Spinach Egg Muffins

Preparation time: 10 minutes
Cooking time: 30 minutes
Servings: 3
Ingredients:
- 5 egg whites
- 2 eggs
- ¼ cup cheddar cheese, shredded
- ¼ cup spinach, chopped
- ¼ cup milk
- 3 lean breakfast turkey sausage

Directions:
1. Preheat the oven to 350°F. Grease muffin tray cups and set aside.

2. In a pan, brown the turkey sausage links over medium-high heat until sausage is brown from all the sides.
3. Cut sausage to ½-inch pieces and set aside.
4. In a large bowl, whisk together eggs, egg whites, milk, pepper, and salt. Stir in spinach.
5. Pour egg mixture into the prepared muffin tray.
6. Divide sausage and cheese evenly between each muffin cup.
7. Bake in preheated oven for 20 minutes or until muffins are set.
8. Serve warm and enjoy it.

Nutrition: calories 120, fat 8, fiber 4, carbs 12, protein 12.

Savoy Cabbage with Coconut Cream Sauce

Preparation time: 5 minutes
Cooking time: 20 minutes
Servings: 4
Ingredients:
- 3 tablespoons olive oil
- 1 onion, chopped
- 4 cloves of garlic, minced
- 1 head savoy cabbage, chopped finely
- 2 cups bone broth
- 1 cup coconut milk freshly squeezed
- 1 bay leaf
- Salt and pepper to taste
- 2 tablespoons chopped parsley

Directions:
1. Heat oil in a pot for 2 minutes.
2. Stir in the onions, bay leaf, and garlic until fragrant, around 3 minutes.
3. Add the rest of the ingredients, except for the parsley, and mix well.
4. Cover pot, bring to a boil, and let it simmer for 5 minutes or until cabbage is tender to taste.
5. Stir in parsley and serve.

Nutrition: Calories: 195; Carbs: 12.3g; Protein: 2.7g; Fat: 19.7

Steamed Squash Chowder

Preparation time: 20 minutes
Cooking time: 40 minutes
Servings: 4
Ingredients:
- 3 cups chicken broth
- 2 tablespoon ghee
- 1 teaspoon chili powder
- ½ teaspoon cumin

- 1 ½ teaspoon salt
- 2 teaspoon cinnamon
- 3 tablespoon olive oil
- 2 carrots, chopped
- 1 small yellow onion, chopped
- 1 green apple sliced and cored
- 1 large butternut squash, peeled, seeded, and chopped to ½-inch cubes

Directions:
1. In a large pot on medium-high fire, melt ghee.
2. Once the ghee is hot, sauté onions for 5 minutes or until soft and translucent.
3. Add olive oil, chili powder, cumin, salt, and cinnamon. Sauté for half a minute.
4. Add chopped squash and apples.
5. Sauté for 10 minutes while stirring once in a while.
6. Add broth, cover, and cook on medium fire for twenty minutes or until apples and squash are tender.
7. With an immersion blender, puree chowder. Adjust consistency by adding more water.
8. Add more salt or pepper depending on desire.
9. Serve and enjoy it.

Nutrition: calories 240, fat 7, fiber 4, carbs 12, protein 12.

CHAPTER 9:
Salads

Prosciutto and Figs Salad

Preparation time: 10 minutes
Cooking time: 0 minutes
Servings: 4
Ingredients:

- One 10–12-ounce package of fresh baby spinach
- 1 small hot red chili pepper, finely diced
- 1 carton figs, stems removed and quartered
- ½ cup walnuts, coarsely chopped
- 1 tablespoon fresh orange juice
- 1 tablespoon honey
- 4 slices prosciutto, cut into strips
- Shaved parmesan cheese for garnish

Directions:

1. Take your spinach and divide them into 4 equal portions. Each portion should be on a separate plate and will act as a base. Add quartered prosciutto, figs, and walnuts on each spinach as toppings.
2. For the dressing, take a small bowl and add honey, orange juice, and diced pepper. Add the mixture over the salad.
3. Finally, toss the salad lightly and use parmesan cheese for the garnish.

Nutrition: calories 190, fat 7, fiber 4, carbs 12, protein 9.

Garden Vegetables and Chickpeas Salad

Preparation time: 10 minutes
Cooking time: 0 minutes
Servings: 4
Ingredients:

- 2 tablespoons freshly squeezed lemon juice
- ⅛ Teaspoon freshly ground pepper
- 1 cup cubed part-skim mozzarella cheese
- 1 tablespoon fresh basil leaf snipped
- 1 (15-ounce) can chickpeas, rinsed and well-drained
- 2 cups coarsely chopped fresh broccoli
- 2 cloves fresh garlic finely minced
- ½ cup sliced fresh carrots
- 1 7½-ounce can diced tomatoes, undrained

Directions:
1. Use a large bowl and add garlic, basil, lemon juice, and ground pepper. Mix them well.
2. Add the chickpeas, carrots, tomatoes with juice, broccoli, and mozzarella cheese. Tops all the ingredients well.
3. You can serve immediately, or you can keep it refrigerated overnight.

Nutrition: calories 140, fat 7, fiber 4, carbs 12, protein 4.

Broccoli Salad Moroccan Style

Preparation Time: 20 minutes
Cooking Time: 0 minutes
Servings: 4
Ingredients:
- ¼ tsp. sea salt
- ¼ tsp. ground cinnamon
- ½ tsp. ground turmeric
- ¾ tsp. ground ginger
- ½ tbsp. extra virgin olive oil
- ½ tbsp. apple cider vinegar
- 2 tbsp. chopped green onion
- 1/3 cup coconut cream
- ½ cup carrots, shredded
- 1 small head of broccoli, chopped

Directions:
1. In a large salad bowl, mix well salt, cinnamon, turmeric, ginger, olive oil, and vinegar.
2. Add remaining ingredients, tossing well to coat.
3. Pop in the ref for at least 30 to 60 minutes before serving.

Nutrition: Calories 90.5, Protein 1.3g, Carbs 4g, Fat 7.7g

Parsley Cheese Balls

Preparation Time: 10 minutes
Cooking time: 1 minute
Servings: 6
Ingredients:
- 1/3 cup Cheddar cheese, shredded
- 1 tablespoon dried dill
- 1 egg, beaten
- ½ teaspoon salt
- 2 tablespoons coconut flakes
- 3 tablespoons sunflower oil

Directions:
Mix up together shredded cheese with dried dill, salt, and coconut flakes.

1. Then add egg and stir carefully until homogenous.
2. After this, make small balls from the cheese mixture. Heat up sunflower oil in the skillet.
3. Place cheese balls in the hot oil and roast them for 10 seconds from each side.
4. Dry the cooked cheese balls with the help of the paper towel.

Nutrition: Calories 105, Fat 10.4, Fiber 0.2, Carbs 0.7, Protein 2.6

Layered Dip

Preparation Time: 10 minutes
Cooking time: 0 minutes
Servings: 12
Ingredients:

- ½ cup hummus
- 8 tablespoons tzatziki
- 1 teaspoon olive oil
- 1 cup tomatoes, chopped
- 1 cup cucumbers, chopped
- 1 tablespoon lemon juice
- 1/3 cup fresh parsley, chopped
- 1 jalapeno pepper, chopped

Directions:
1. In the mixing bowl, mix up together fresh parsley, lemon juice, olive oil, cucumbers, tomatoes, and chopped jalapeno pepper.
2. Then make the layer of ½ part of tomato mixture in the casserole mold or glass mold.
3. Top it with the layer of hummus.
4. Then add the remaining tomato mixture and flatten it well. Top it with tzatziki and flatten well. Store the dip in the fridge for up to 3 hours.

Nutrition: Calories 49, Fat 3.6, Fiber 1, Carbs 3.3, Protein 1.1.

Avocado Chicken Salad

Preparation time: 10 minutes
Cooking time: 30 minutes
Servings: 2
Ingredients:

- Cooked chicken (2 cups/10 oz. - lean)
- 2% Plain Greek yogurt (0.5 cup - lean)
- Avocado (3 oz. - healthy fat)
- Garlic powder (0.5 tsp. - condiment)
- Salt (0.25 tsp. - condiment)
- Pepper (1/8 tsp. - condiment)
- Lime juice (1 tbsp. + 1 tsp. - condiment)
- Fresh cilantro (0.25 cup - condiment)

Direction:

1. Finely dice the chicken and measure it (cooked). Chop the avocado and cilantro.
2. Toss each of the fixings into a mixing container and pop it in the fridge until serving time.
3. Portion the delicious treat into two dishes and serve with your favorite green option.

Nutrition: calories 140, fat 7, fiber 4, carbs 12, protein 4.

Tunisian Style Carrot Salad

Preparation time: 15 minutes
Cooking time: 0 minutes
Servings: 6
Ingredients:
- 10 medium carrots peeled and sliced
- 1 cup crumbled feta cheese, divided
- 2 teaspoons caraway seed
- ¼ cup extra-virgin olive oil
- 6 tablespoons apple cider vinegar
- 5 teaspoons freshly minced garlic
- 1 tablespoon Harissa paste (choose the level of heat based on your preference)
- 20 pitted Kalamata olives, reserving some for garnish
- Salt to taste

Directions:
1. Take out a medium saucepan and place it on medium heat. Fill it with water and add the carrots. Cook carrots until tender. Drain and cool the carrots under cold water. Drain again to remove any excess water.
2. Take out a large bowl and place the carrots in them.
3. Take out a mortar and combine salt, garlic, and caraway seeds. Grind them until they form a paste. Otherwise, you can also use a small bowl, preferably one not made out of glass, for the grind. The final option would be to toss the ingredients into a blender and pulse them.
4. Add vinegar and Harissa into the bowl with the carrots and mix them well.
5. Use a large spoon and mash the carrots. Add the garlic mixture into the carrot and mix again until they have all blended well. Add the olive oil and mix again.
6. Finally, add about ½ the feta cheese and all the olives and mix well again.
7. Take out a large bowl and add the salad to it. Top it with the remaining feta cheese.

Nutrition: calories 140, fat 7, fiber 4, carbs 12, protein 4.

Beef Taco Salad

Preparation time: 10 minutes
Cooking time: 30 minutes
Servings: 1
Ingredients:
- 95 to 97% lean ground beef - 4.5 oz. when cooked (6.5 oz. - ¾ leaner -lean)
- Low-sodium taco seasoning mix (1.5 tsp. - condiment)

- Water (2 tbsp.)
- Lettuce - chopped (2 cups - greens)
- Tomatoes (0.5 cup - greens)
- 2% Reduced-fat Mexican Cheese (1 oz./0.25 cup - ¼ of 1 lean)
- Hidden Valley Light Ranch Dressing (2 tbsp. - healthy fat)

Direction:
1. Prep the veggies by chopping the lettuce and tomatoes; set them aside for now.
2. Warm a skillet to cook the beef. Drain the fat and toss back into the pan. Pour in the seasoning mix and water. Simmer for about five minutes.
3. Serve as desired with the meat over the bed of lettuce and tomatoes.
4. Dust it using the Mexican cheese and dressing.

Nutrition: calories 160, fat 8, fiber 2, carbs 6, protein 3.

Garden Salad with Oranges and Olives

Preparation Time: 10 minutes
Cooking Time: 15 minutes
Servings: 4
Ingredients:

- ½ cup red wine vinegar
- 1 tbsp. extra virgin olive oil
- 1 tbsp. finely chopped celery
- 1 tbsp. finely chopped red onion
- 16 large ripe black olives
- 2 garlic cloves
- 2 navel oranges, peeled and segmented
- 4 boneless, skinless chicken breasts, 4-oz each
- 4 garlic cloves, minced
- 8 cups leaf lettuce washed and dried
- Cracked black pepper to taste

Directions:
1. Prepare the dressing by mixing the pepper, celery, onion, olive oil, garlic, and vinegar in a small bowl. Whisk well to combine.
2. Lightly grease grate and preheat grill to high.
3. Rub chicken with the garlic cloves and discard garlic.
4. Grill chicken for 5 minutes per side or until cooked through.
5. Remove from grill and let it stand for 5 minutes before cutting into ½-inch strips.
6. In 4 serving plates, evenly arrange two cups lettuce, ¼ of the sliced oranges, and 4 olives per plate.
7. Top each plate with ¼ serving of grilled chicken, evenly drizzle with dressing, serve and enjoy it.

Nutrition: Calories 259.8, Protein 48.9g, Carbs 12.9g, Fat 1.4g

North African Zucchini Salad

Preparation time: 10 minutes
Cooking time: 0 minutes
Servings: 4
Ingredients:

- 1 pound firm green zucchini thinly sliced
- ½ teaspoon ground cumin
- 2 cloves fresh garlic, finely minced
- Juice from 1 large lemon
- 1 tablespoon extra-virgin olive oil
- 1½ tablespoons plain low-fat yogurt
- Crumbled feta cheese
- Finely chopped parsley for garnish
- Salt and freshly ground pepper to taste

Directions:
1. Add the zucchini into a large saucepan and steam it for about 2–5 minutes, or until it becomes tender and crispy. Place the zucchini under cold water and drain well.
2. Take out a large bowl and mix cumin, olive oil, lemon juice, garlic, and yogurt. Add salt and pepper to taste.
3. Add the zucchini into the mixture in the bowl and toss gently.
4. Serve with feta cheese and parsley as garnish.

Nutrition: calories 140, fat 6, fiber 4, carbs 8.2, protein 2.

Spanish Salad

Preparation time: 10 minutes
Cooking time: 0 minutes
Servings: 6
Ingredients:

- 2 bunches romaine lettuce, cleaned and trimmed
- 1 large sweet onion thinly sliced
- 3 medium ripe tomatoes, chopped
- 3 tablespoons balsamic vinegar
- ¼ cup extra-virgin olive oil
- 1 red bell pepper, seeded and thinly sliced
- 1 green bell pepper, seeded and thinly sliced
- ¼ cup chopped and pitted black olives
- ¼ cup chopped and pitted marinated green olives
- Salt and freshly ground pepper to taste

Directions:
1. Take out 6 plates and place romaine lettuce on them to form a base.
2. Add peppers, tomatoes, onion, and olives on top of each of the lettuce bases.

3. In a small bowl, combine olive oil and vinegar together. Add the dressing over the salad.
4. Add salt and pepper to taste, if preferred.

Nutrition: calories 140, fat 7, fiber 4, carbs 12, protein 4.

Parsley Couscous Salad

Preparation time: 2 hours
Cooking time: 0 minutes
Servings: 4
Ingredients:

- ¼ cup couscous
- 2 teaspoons extra-virgin olive oil
- ¼ cup of water
- 2 teaspoons lemon zest
- 1 medium ripe tomato, peeled, seeded, and diced
- 2 tablespoons pine nuts
- 2 tablespoons fresh lemon juice
- ¼ cup finely chopped fresh flat parsley leaves
- 2 tablespoons finely chopped fresh mint leaves
- 2 heads Belgian endive, leaves for scooping
- Whole wheat pita rounds, cut into wedges and toasted until crispy
- Salt and freshly ground pepper to taste

Directions:

1. Take out a medium bowl and then combine lemon juice and water. All the mixture to stand for about 1 hour.
2. After the hour, add mint, parsley, lemon zest, olive oil, and pine nuts. Mix the ingredients well.
3. Add the couscous to the mixture. Allow it to stand for about 1 hour. After 1 hour, add salt and pepper to taste.
4. Place couscous mixture in the center of a plate and top it with tomato. You can surround the couscous salad with toasted pita wedges and endive leaves, which makes for a wonderful presentation.
5. Refrigerator overnight so that you can have it the next day.

Nutrition: calories 120, fat 7, fiber 1, carbs 12, protein 5.

Grilled Tempeh Sticks

Preparation Time: 5 minutes
Cooking time: 8 minutes
Servings: 6
Ingredients:

- 11 oz. soy tempeh
- 1 teaspoon olive oil
- ½ teaspoon ground black pepper

- ¼ teaspoon garlic powder

Directions:
1. Cut soy tempeh into the sticks.
2. Sprinkle every tempeh stick with ground black pepper, garlic powder, and olive oil.
3. Preheat the grill to 375°F.
4. Place the tempeh sticks in the grill and cook them for 4 minutes from each side. The time of cooking depends on the tempeh sticks size.
5. The cooked tempeh sticks will have a light brown color.

Nutrition: Calories 88, Fat 2.5, Fiber 3.6, Carbs 10.2, Protein 6.5.

Avocado Salad

Preparation time: 10 minutes
Cooking time: 0 minutes
Servings: 3
Ingredients:

- 1 small onion, finely chopped
- 1 large ripe avocado pitted and peeled
- 2 tablespoons chopped fresh parsley
- 2 teaspoons fresh lime juice
- ½ small hot pepper, finely chopped (optional)
- 1 cup halved cherry tomatoes
- Salt and freshly ground pepper to taste

Directions:
1. Start with the avocado and cut it into bite-sized pieces.
2. Add parsley, lime juice, tomatoes, onion, and hot pepper. Mix all the ingredients well. Add salt and pepper to taste.
3. Finally, add the avocado into the mixture and mix them well.

Nutrition: calories 130, fat 8, fiber 4, carbs 12, protein 2.

Peppered Watercress Salad

Preparation time: 5 minutes
Cooking time: 0 minutes
Servings: 4
Ingredients:

- 2 teaspoons champagne vinegar
- 2 bunches (about 8 cups) watercress, rinsed and rough stems removed
- 2 tablespoons extra-virgin olive oil
- Salt and freshly ground pepper to taste

Directions:
1. Drain the watercress properly.

2. Take out a small bowl and then add salt, pepper, vinegar, and olive oil. Mix them well together.
3. Transfer the watercress to a bowl. Add the vinegar mixture into it and toss it well.
4. Serve immediately.

Nutrition: calories 80, fat 7, fiber 4, carbs 1, protein 4.

Caprese Salad

Preparation time: 10 minutes
Cooking time: 30 minutes
Servings: 4
Ingredients:
- Fresh mozzarella (4 oz. - 1 lean)
- Baby spinach (1 cup - greens)
- Roma or heirloom tomatoes (1 cup/180g - greens)
- Fresh basil (0.25 cup - condiment)
- Black pepper & salt (1/8 tsp. each - condiments)
- Walden Farms Balsamic Vinaigrette Dressing (2 tbsp. - condiment)

Directions:
1. Slice the tomatoes and chop the basil. Cube the mozzarella.
2. Arrange the spinach greens on a plate and add the tomatoes, pepper, and salt.
3. Drizzle with the dressing and cheese with a sprinkling of fresh basil to serve.

Note: The mozzarella should contain 3–6 grams of fat per ounce.
Nutrition: calories 90, fat 8, fiber 3, carbs 10, protein 2.

Caesar Salad

Preparation time: 5 minutes
Cooking time: 0 minutes
Servings: 6
Ingredients:
- 10 small pitted black olives, chopped
- 1–2 bunches romaine lettuce, cleaned and torn in pieces
- 2 teaspoons lemon juice
- 2½ teaspoons balsamic vinegar
- ½ cup grated parmesan cheese
- ½ cup non-fat plain yogurt
- 1 teaspoon Worcestershire sauce
- ½ teaspoon anchovy paste
- 2 cloves freshly minced garlic

Directions:
1. Take out a large bowl and place romaine lettuce in it.

2. Take out your blender and add mix lemon juice, yogurt, garlic, anchovy paste, vinegar, Worcestershire sauce, and ¼ cup parmesan cheese. Mix all the ingredients well until they are smooth.
3. Pour the yogurt mixture over the lettuce and toss lightly.
4. Top the salad with the remaining parmesan cheese.

Nutrition: calories 140, fat 7, fiber 4, carbs 4, protein 4.

Cress and Tangerine Salad

Preparation time: 15 minutes
Cooking time: 0 minutes
Servings: 4
Ingredients:
- 4 large sweet tangerines
- ¼ cup extra-virgin olive oil
- 2 large bunches watercress, washed and stems removed
- Juice from 1 fresh lemon
- 10 cherry tomatoes, halved
- 16 pitted Kalamata olives
- Sea salt and freshly ground pepper to taste

Directions:
1. Take the tangerines and peel them into a medium-sized bowl. Make sure that you remove any pits and squeeze the sections. You should have around ¼ cup of tangerine juice. Set sections aside.
2. Take a large bowl and add lemon juice, tangerine juice, and olive oil. Mix them together and add salt and pepper for flavor, if you prefer.
3. Use paper towels to pat the cress dry. Add watercress, tomatoes, and olives to the bowl containing the tangerine sections (not to be confused with the bowl containing tangerine juice). Toss them lightly.
4. Pour the tangerine juice mixture on top. Mix well and serve.

Nutrition: calories 140, fat 7, fiber 4, carbs 12, protein 4.

CHAPTER 10:
Sandwiches

White Bean Soup with Turkey Sausage and Kale
Preparation time: 10 minutes
Cooking time: 30 minutes
Servings: 4
Ingredients:

- 2 extra virgin olive oil spoons
- 1 onion, Cut
- 1 clove of garlic, chopped
- 1 1/4 pounds lean turkey sausage, cut casings
- 6 cups chicken broth with low-sodium content
- 1 cup white canned beans, rinsed and drained
- 1 cup finely chopped kale, salt, and ground black pepper, to taste

Directions:

1. Warm oil over medium-high heat in a medium heavy-duty pot. Add garlic and onion, then sauté for 2 to 3 minutes. Use sausage to break the meat into small pieces, using a wooden spoon. Stir in constantly for 5 to 6 minutes, until the meat is cooked through.
2. Stir in broth and beans for the chicken. Cover with a lid and simmer for 10 minutes on low heat.
3. Attach the kale and continue to simmer for another 10 minutes, protected with the brush.
4. Season with salt and pepper, and then divide the soup into 4 serving bowls.

Nutrition: Calories 211, Fat 7, Fiber 1, Carbs 12, Protein 4.

Chicken Salad Sandwiches
Preparation time: 10 minutes
Cooking time: 30 minutes
Servings: 4
Ingredients:

- 1 stalk celery, finely chopped
- 1 spoonful finely chopped onion
- 1 pound of pine nuts
- 1 teaspoon spicy brown mustard
- 1 teaspoon fat-free sour cream
- Teaspoon fat-free plain yogurt, shake with salt and black pepper
- (3-ounce) chunk chicken cans, rinsed twice, and drained

- Four slices whole-grain bread
- 2 leaves Lettuce

Directions:
1. Put celery, onion, pine nuts, mustard, sour cream, yogurt, salt, and pepper in a bowl; whisk for the mix. Attach chicken, and blend well using a fork.
2. Make the sandwiches by breaking the chicken salad between two slices of bread. Top each with 1 lettuce leaf and a slice of bread leftover.

Nutrition: Calories 101, Fat 6, Fiber 2, Carbs 12, Protein 3.

Avocado-Egg Salad Sandwich

Preparation time: 10 minutes
Cooking time: 30 minutes
Servings: 4
Ingredients:

- 2 Hard-boiled eggs, peeled
- Half-average avocado, washed, pitted, and cut into 1/2"
- 1 x 2% Greek yogurt
- 1/2 tsp. mustard Dijon
- 1/2 tbs. of fresh chives Salt and ground black pepper, to taste
- 12 thin slices of cucumber
- 4 slices of whole-grain bread, grilled

Directions:
1. The egg yolks are isolated from the egg whites. Add the yolks, avocado, cream, mustard, chives, salt, and pepper in a small cup. And bash with a fork.
2. Break the egg whites and stir in a mixture of yolks.
3. Divide the cucumber into 2 slices of bread. On the plate, spoon egg salad and close with the top half of the plate. Cut half of the sandwiches, and serve.

Nutrition: Calories 101, Fat 6, Fiber 2, Carbs 12, Protein 3.

Italian Sloppy Joe

Preparation time: 10 minutes
Cooking time: 30 minutes
Servings: 4
Ingredients:

- 1 pound of lean Italian turkey sausage, cut casings
- Cut 1/2 cup onion
- 3 Garlic cloves, minced
- 1 Red bell potato seeded and cut into 1/2-inch pieces
- 1 Green bell pepper, seeded and chopped in 1/2" bits
- 1 1/3 cups of crushed tomato canned
- 1/2 cup of dried rosemary
- Salt and black chili pepper, to taste

- 4 100-calories, whole-wheat potato rolls
- 4 Low-fat provolone cheese slices
- 1 cup baby spinach

Directions:

1. Heat a broad skillet over medium-high heat, without sticking. Use sausage to break the meat into small pieces, using a wooden spoon. Stir in constantly for 5 to 6 minutes, until the meat is cooked through.

2. Stir in garlic and onion. Switch sausage mixture to slow cooker bowl after cooking for around 2 minutes. Connect the onions, tomatoes, salt, rosemary, and pepper. Stir to blend.

3. Place a lid over the slow cooker and set the heat to medium. Cook 4 hours.

4. Fill a roll with a 1/2 cup of meat heaping up to serve. Top with spinach

Nutrition: Calories 101, Fat 6, Fiber 2, Carbs 12, Protein 3.

Turkey Taco Lettuce Wraps

Preparation time: 10 minutes
Cooking time: 30 minutes
Servings: 4
Ingredients:

- 1 pound 93% lean ground turkey
- 1 Teaspoon powdered garlic
- 1 Teaspoon cumin in the field
- 1 Tablespoon of chili powder
- Ri1 Teaspoon of paprika
- 1/2 cup of dried oregano
- Salt and black chili pepper, to taste
- 1/2 Little Onion, Sliced
- 1/4 Red bell pepper chopped and seeded
- 1/2 cup tomato canned sauce
- 8 Big, washed and dried iceberg leaves
- Cut 1/2 cup fresh cilantro

Directions

1. Heat a broad skillet over medium-high heat, without sticking. Using a wooden spoon to split the meat into small pieces, and add the ground turkey to the skillet. Cook, constantly stirring, for 4 to 5 minutes until the meat is no longer pink.

2. Incorporate garlic, cumin, chili powder, paprika, oregano, salt, and pepper. Stir in onion, pepper bell, and tomato sauce. Use a lid to cover the skillet, reduce heat to medium, and simmer for 20 minutes.

3. Place 2 slices of lettuce on each plate to eat. Divide filling between leaves of lettuce, putting each leaf in the middle. Garnish, and serve with cilantro.

Nutrition: Calories 201, Fat 6, Fiber 2, Carbs 7, Protein 9.

Tomato Finger Sandwich

Preparation Time: 10 minutes
Cooking time: 0 minutes
Servings: 6
Ingredients:

- 6 corn tortillas
- 1 tablespoon cream cheese
- 1 tablespoon ricotta cheese
- ½ teaspoon minced garlic
- 1 tablespoon fresh dill, chopped
- 2 tomatoes, sliced

Directions:

1. Cut every tortilla into 2 triangles.
2. Then mix up together cream cheese, ricotta cheese, minced garlic, and dill.
3. Spread 6 triangles with cream cheese mixture.
4. Then place a sliced tomato on them and cover with remaining tortilla triangles.

Nutrition: Calories 71, Fat 1.6, Fiber 2.1, Carbs 12.8, Protein 2.3

Slow-cooker French Dip Sandwiches

Preparation time: 10 minutes
Cooking time: 30 minutes
Servings: 4
Ingredients:

- 1 tbsp. hairy garlic
- 1 tbsp. cut fresh rosemary
- Tbsp. new thyme leaves black pepper and salt to taste
- Pound lean round roast beef, fat trimmed
- Tsp. Worcestershire Sauce
- (14.5-ounce) tins of low sodium beef broth, plus more if required
- Big, sliced onions
- 1 Big red potatoes, seeded and cut into strips
- Big green potatoes, seeded and cut into strips
- Baguettes (8-Ounce)
- 8 Slices of mozzarella with reduced-fat

Directions:

1. Combine the garlic, rosemary, thyme, salt, and pepper in a small cup. Rub the spice mix absolutely with the roast and put it in the slow cooker.
2. Add sauce from Worcestershire and enough broth to cover the beef. Cover with lid and cook at medium, depending on roast thickness, until the meat is a fork-tender, 9 to 12 hours.
3. Add the onions and bell peppers into the slow cooker one hour before the meat is cooked. Move the meat to a cutting board when roasting is tender, and shred with a fork or slice with a knife.

4. Then extract the onions and peppers from the broth using a slotted spoon. Use a gravy separator to extract any fat from the broth, or leave it overnight in the refrigerator to skim off the solid fat.

5. Preheat the broiler to serve. With 2 ounces of beef, plus onions, peppers, and cheese, slice baguette on end. Place under the broiler until cheese melts, and serve for dipping with broth ramekins.

Nutrition: Calories 101, Fat 6, Fiber 2, Carbs 12, Protein 3.

Egg & Cheese Bagel Sandwich

Preparation time: 10 minutes
Cooking time: 30 minutes
Servings: 4
Ingredients:

- 1 slice reduced-fat cheddar cheese
- 1 egg
- 1 teaspoon bagel seasoning
- Cooking Spray
- 3 tablespoons cold water
- 1 Sachet Optavia select buttermilk cheddar herb biscuit

Directions:

1. Preheat your oven to 350°F.

2. Combine water and biscuit and mix very well before diving the mixture equally in 2 slots of the donut pan. Drizzle the top with seasoning and bake for 12–15 minutes when the edges should have become golden brown.

3. Get a lightly greased skillet to cook the egg.

4. Top 1 of the "bagel" piece with egg and cheese and egg before topping it with the other "bagel" piece.

Nutrition: Calories 95, Fat 5, Fiber 6, Carbs 5, Protein 4.

CHAPTER 11:
Lean Meat

Teriyaki Pork Stir-Fry

Preparation time: 15 minutes
Cooking time: 15 minutes
Servings: 4
Ingredients:

- 1 lb. pork loin, cut into thin strips
- 2 tbsp. olive oil, divided
- 1 tsp. garlic, minced
- 1 tsp. fresh ginger, minced
- 2 tbsp. low-sodium soy sauce
- 1 tbsp. fresh lemon juice
- 1 tbsp. Erythritol
- 1 tsp. arrowroot starch
- 10 oz. broccoli florets
- 1 carrot, peeled and sliced
- 1 large red bell pepper seeded and cut into strips
- 2 Scallions cut into 2-inch pieces

Direction:
1. In a bowl, mix well pork strips, ½ tbsp. olive oil, garlic, and ginger.
2. For the sauce, add the soy sauce, lemon juice, Erythritol, and arrowroot starch in a small bowl and mix well.
3. Heat the remaining olive oil in a large non-stick skillet over high heat and sear the pork strips for about 3–4 minutes or until cooked through.
4. With a slotted spoon, transfer the pork into a bowl.
5. In the same skillet, add the carrot and cook for about 2–3 minutes.
6. Add the broccoli, bell pepper, and scallion and cook, covered for about 1–2 minutes.
7. Stir the cooked pork and sauce, and stir fry and cook for about 3–5 minutes or until the desired doneness, stirring occasionally.
8. Remove from the heat and serve.

Nutrition: Calories361, Fat 6, Fiber 2, Carbs 10, Protein 34.

Adobo Sirloin

Preparation time: 10 minutes
Cooking time: 30 minutes
Servings: 1
Ingredients:

- 1 lime juice
- 1 tbsp. chopped garlic
- 1 tbs. dried oregano
- Teaspoon cumin
- Tablespoons finely chopped chipotle chilies in adobo sauce plus 2 spoonfuls of sauce
- 4 Sirloin steaks (6-ounce), trimmed with fat
- Salt and black chili pepper, to taste

Directions:
1. Combine the lime juice, garlic, oregano, cumin, chilies, and adobo sauce in a small cup. Healthy balance to blend.
2. Season with salt and pepper to taste. Put steaks with adobo marinade into a big Ziploc container. Seal tightly and cover. Refrigerate, trembling slightly, for at least 2 hours.
3. Prepare a grill to heat high. Cover the barbecue grills loosely with a cooking spray. Once the grill is heated, cook steaks on each side for about 4 to 5 minutes, until the desired doneness. Give the steaks 10 minutes to rest and serve.

Nutrition: Calories2 49, Fat 10, Fiber 1, Carbs 8, Protein 30.

Asian Inspired Beef

Preparation time: 15 minutes
Cooking time: 20 minutes
Servings: 4
Ingredients:

- 16 oz. sirloin steak trimmed and cut into thin strips
- Salt and freshly ground black pepper, to taste
- 2 tbsp. olive oil, divided
- 2 garlic cloves, minced
- 1 Serrano pepper, seeded and chopped finely
- 2 cup broccoli florets
- 2 tbsp. low-sodium soy sauce
- 2 tbsp. fresh lime juice

Directions:
1. Season the steak slices with black pepper.
2. Heat 1 tbsp. of oil in a large skillet over medium heat and cook the steak slices for about 6–8 minutes or until browned from all sides.
3. With a slotted spoon, transfer the steak slices onto a plate.
4. Heat remaining oil in the same skillet over medium heat and sauté the garlic and Serrano pepper for about 1 minute.
5. Add the broccoli and stir fry for about 2–3 minutes.
6. Stir in the cooked steak slices, soy sauce, and lime juice and cook for about 3–4 minutes.
7. Serve hot.

Nutrition: Calories291, Fat 6, Fiber 2, Carbs 6, Protein 20.

Beef Stroganoff

Preparation time: 10 minutes
Cooking time: 30 minutes
Servings: 1
Ingredients:

- Salt and black chili pepper, to taste
- 8 oz. egg noodles
- Trimmed with fat and a sliced pound of beef
- Tbs. of extra virgin olive oil
- 1/2 sliced onion
- 4 ounces white, sliced mushrooms
- 1 tbs. of cornstarch
- 1 (10.5-ounce) can condense, divided beef broth
- 1 tsp. Mustard Dijon
- 1 garlic clove, minced and peeled
- 3 spoonfuls white wine
- 1/2 tbs. Worcestershire Sauce
- 2 Spoonfuls low-fat sour cream
- 2 tbsp. cream cheese with reduced-fat

Directions:

1. Pick up a big pot of lightly salted water over high heat to a boil. Cook noodles as indicated on the box. Drain, and set aside.
2. In the meantime, season salt and peppered beef. Heat oil over medium heat in a large skillet. Add beef; brown on all sides, then force one side of the saucepan.
3. Add the onion and mushrooms, and cook for around 3 to 5 minutes until tender. Move beef to the left. Combine cornstarch and 2 tablespoons of cold beef broth in a small tub. Apply to the skillet and whisk to deglaze with the juices in the pan.
4. Pour the remainder of the beef broth down. Bring to a boil, with regular stirring. Reduce to low heat and stir in mustard, garlic, and Wine, and Sauce from Worcestershire. Cover with a tight cap, and cook for 10 minutes.
5. Stir in sour cream and cream cheese, two minutes until the beef is cooked. Remove well, and allow the beef to finish the sauce cooking. Let meat rest for five minutes, and serve

Nutrition: Calories 549, Fat 10, Fiber 1, Carbs 8, Protein 33.

Beef lo Mein

Preparation time: 10 minutes
Cooking time: 30 minutes
Servings: 1
Ingredients:

- Salt, enough to taste
- 2 oz. full-grain spaghetti

- 1 tbsp. sesame oil
- 1 Sirloin steak (6-ounce), fat trimmed, and cut into strips
- 1/4 cup fresh pea pods, cut
- 1/4 cup broccoli blossoms
- One and a half cup shredded carrots
- Scallion, hammered
- 1/8 Red pepper flakes in a teaspoon
- 1/2 garlic clove, minced and peeled
- Tablespoon soy sauce with less sodium
- 1/2 teaspoon of fresh ginger peeled and grated
- 1 Teaspoon of brushed sesame seeds

Directions:
1. Bring a medium pot of lightly salted water up over high heat to a boil. Cook spaghetti as instructed on the box. Drain, and set aside.
2. In the meantime, over medium-high heat, steam oil in a wok or large skillet. Connect the beef and stir-fry, about 4 to 6 minutes until brown. Delete, and set aside from the pan.
3. Add snow peas, broccoli, cabbage, scallion, and garlic. Stir-fry for 2 to 3 minutes.
4. Add soy sauce, ginger, reserved noodles, and beef to taste. Nice mix and cook until hot.
5. Remove wok from heat and garnish with sesame seeds to stir-fry.

Nutrition: Calories749, Fat 17, Fiber 1, Carbs 8, Protein 70.

Mexican Beef Bowl

Preparation time: 15 minutes
Cooking time: 15 minutes
Servings: 4
Ingredients:

- 1 tsp. red chili powder
- 1 tsp. ground cumin
- Salt and freshly ground black pepper, to taste
- 1 lb. flank steak, trimmed
- 2 scallions
- 1 lime cut in half
- 8 cup lettuce, torn
- 1 red bell pepper, seeded and sliced
- 1 cup tomato, chopped
- 1 jalapeño pepper, chopped
- ½ cup fresh cilantro, chopped
- ¼ cup light sour cream

Directions:
1. Preheat the grill to medium-high heat. Grease the grill grate.
2. In a small bowl, mix together the spices, salt, and black pepper.

3. Rub the steak with spice mixture generously.
4. Place the steak onto the grill and cook for about 4–6 minutes per side or until desired doneness.
5. Remove from the grill and place the steak onto a cutting board for about 5 minutes.
6. Now, place the scallions onto the grill and cook for about 1 minute per side.
7. Place the lime halves onto the grill, cut-side down, and cook for about 1 minute.
8. Remove the scallions and lime halves from the grill and place onto a plate.
9. Chop the scallions roughly.
10. With a sharp knife, cut the steak into thin slices.
11. In a bowl, place the beef slices and chopped scallions.
12. Squeeze the lime halves over steak mixture and toss to coat well.
13. Divide lettuce into serving bowls and top each with bell pepper, followed by tomato, jalapeño pepper, cilantro, and beef mixture.
14. Top each bowl with sour cream and serve

Nutrition: Calories 101, Fat 6, Fiber 2, Carbs 12, Protein 3.

Weeknight Dinner Meal

Preparation time: 15 minutes
Cooking time: 15 minutes
Servings: 4
Ingredients:
For Beef:
- 4 (6-oz.) beef tenderloin fillets
- Salt and freshly ground black pepper, to taste
- 2 tbsp. olive oil, divided
- 1 tsp. garlic, smashed
- 1 tbsp. fresh thyme, chopped

For Mushrooms:
- 2 tbsp. olive oil
- 1 lb. fresh mushrooms, sliced
- 2 tsp. garlic, smashed
- Salt and freshly ground black pepper, to taste

Directions:
For beef:
1. Season the beef fillets with salt and black pepper evenly and set aside.
2. In a cast-iron skillet, heat the oil over medium heat and sauté the garlic and thyme for about 1 minute.
3. Add the fillets and cook for about 5–7 minutes per side.
4. Meanwhile, for mushrooms: in another cast-iron skillet, heat the oil over medium heat and cook the mushrooms, garlic, salt, and black pepper for about 7–8 minutes, stirring frequently.
5. Divide the fillets onto serving plates.
6. Top with mushroom mixture and serve.

Nutrition: Calories 401, Fat 26, Fiber 2, Carbs 4.2, Protein 53.

Filling Beef Dish

Preparation time: 10 minutes
Cooking time: 12 minutes
Servings: 4

Ingredients:

- 2 tbsp. olive oil
- 4 garlic cloves, minced
- 1 lb. beef sirloin steak, cut into bite-sized pieces
- Freshly ground black pepper, to taste
- 1½ cup carrots, peeled and cut into matchsticks
- 1½ cup fresh kale, tough ribs removed and chopped.
- 3 tbsp. low-sodium soy sauce

Directions:

1. In a skillet, heat the oil over medium heat and sauté the garlic for about 1 minute.
2. Add the beef and black pepper and stir to combine.
3. Increase the heat to medium-high and cook for about 3–4 minutes or until browned from all sides.
4. Add the carrot, kale, and soy sauce and cook for about 4–5 minutes.
5. Stir in the black pepper and remove from the heat.

Nutrition: Calories 311, Fat 6, Fiber 2, Carbs 12, Protein 27.

CHAPTER 12:
Optavia Recipes

Super-Delicious Avocado
Preparation time: 10 minutes
Cooking time: 15 minutes
Servings: 4
Ingredients:
- 1 cup cooked chicken, shredded
- 1 avocado halved and pitted
- 1 tbsp. fresh lime juice
- ¼ cup yellow onion, chopped finely
- ¼ cup low-fat plain Greek yogurt
- 1 tsp. Dijon mustard
- Pinch of cayenne pepper
- Salt and freshly ground black pepper, to taste

Directions:
1. With a spoon, scoop out the flesh from the middle of each avocado half and transfer into a bowl.
2. Add the lime juice and mash until well combined.
3. Add remaining ingredients and stir to combine.
4. Divide the chicken mixture into avocado halves evenly and serve immediately.

Nutrition: Calories 2811, Fat 6, Fiber 2, Carbs 12, Protein 23

Baked Chicken and Zucchini Casserole
Preparation time: 10 minutes
Cooking time: 10 minutes
Servings: 4
Ingredients:
- 1 ¾ pounds boneless chicken breast
- ¼ teaspoon garlic powder
- ¼ teaspoon salt
- ¼ teaspoon pepper
- 4 teaspoons olive oil
- 1 cup diced zucchini
- 1 cup diced tomatoes
- 1 teaspoon basil leaves
- 1 teaspoon oregano
- 1 cup part-skim mozzarella cheese

Directions:
1. Butterfly the chicken slices in half to make four thin pieces.
2. Season with garlic powder, salt, and pepper.
3. Heat skillet over medium flame and add oil.
4. Brown the chicken slices in olive oil for 3 minutes on each side. Place the chicken in a baking dish. Set aside.
5. To the same skillet, sauté the zucchini in the pan until soft, then add the tomatoes, basil, and oregano. Season with more salt and pepper to taste.
6. Pour vegetable over chicken and top with mozzarella cheese.
7. Bake for 20 minutes in a 350°F preheated oven.

Nutrition: Calories 365, Fat 10, Fiber 2, Carbs 16, Protein 53.

Chicken Rice

Preparation time: 10 minutes
Cooking time: 30 minutes
Servings: 4
Ingredients:

- 1 ¾ pound boneless chicken breast
- ¼ teaspoon salt and pepper
- 2 garlic cloves, minced
- 1 scallion, minced
- 4 cups cauliflower, grated
- 1 ½ cups cherry tomatoes, halved
- 40 green olives, pitted
- ½ cup green beans, cut into ¼ inch pieces

Directions:
1. Preheat the oven to 350°F.
2. Season the chicken with salt and pepper. Place on a greased baking sheet.
3. Roast the chicken for 20 minutes. Remove from the oven and set aside.
4. Meanwhile, mix all ingredients in a pot and simmer on low for 10 minutes.
5. Serve the cauliflower rice with the chicken.

Nutrition: Calories 315, Fat 10, Fiber 2, Carbs 16, Protein 33.

Mexican Turkey Soup

Preparation time: 10 minutes
Cooking time: 30 minutes
Servings: 4
Ingredients:

- ¼ cup olive oil
- 1 jalapeno, seeds removed, then chopped
- 1 cup cilantro, chopped
- 2 cups green onions, finely chopped

- 3 cloves of garlic, minced
- 1 cup red bell pepper, seeded and chopped
- 1 teaspoon dried oregano
- ½ teaspoon cayenne pepper
- Salt and pepper to taste
- 12 ounces turkey breast, sliced
- 6 Roma tomatoes, chopped
- 2 cups chicken stock
- 2 cups tomato sauce

Directions:
1. Heat oil in a large pot and add the jalapeno, green onion, cilantro, garlic, bell pepper, oregano, cayenne pepper. Season with salt and pepper to taste. Cook for 10 minutes on low heat.
2. Add the turkey and cook for another 3 minutes before stirring in the tomatoes.
3. Add the remaining ingredients.
4. Bring to a boil for 10 minutes.
5. Remove from the heat and serve

Nutrition: Calories 335, Fat 10, Fiber 2, Carbs 16, Protein 33.

Tuna Boats
Preparation time: 10 minutes
Cooking time: 15 minutes
Servings: 4
Ingredients:

- 1 large avocado, halved and pitted
- 1 tbsp. onion, chopped finely
- 2 tbsp. fresh lemon juice
- 5 oz. cooked tuna, chopped
- Freshly ground black pepper, to taste

Directions:
1. With a spoon, scoop out the flesh from the middle of each avocado half and transfer into a bowl.
2. Add the onion and lemon juice and mash until well combined.
3. Add tuna, salt and black pepper and stir to combine.
4. Divide the tuna mixture into both avocado halves evenly and serve immediately

Nutrition: Calories 101, Fat 6, Fiber 2, Carbs 12, Protein 3.

Philly Cheesesteak Stuffed Peppers
Preparation time: 10 minutes
Cooking time: 60 minutes
Servings: 4

Ingredients:
- 4 medium green bell peppers, sliced on top and seeded
- 1/3 cup diced yellow onion
- 2 garlic cloves, minced
- ¼ cup low sodium has been broth
- 6 ounces baby Bella mushrooms, sliced
- 1-pound shaved deli roast beef
- 4 tablespoons low-fat cream cheese
- 4 ounces reduced-fat provolone cheese

Directions:
1. Preheat the oven to 400°F.
2. Set aside the bell pepper and make sure that they are clean inside.
3. In a skillet, sauté the onion and garlic in broth over medium flame for 5 minutes. Add the mushrooms and deli beef. Stir to cook everything.
4. Remove from skillet and stir in the cream cheese.
5. Line each of the bell pepper with a quarter slice of cheese, fill an eighth with the roast beef mixture, and top with cheese.
6. Place in the oven and bake for 20 minutes.

Nutrition: Calories 481, Fat 6, Fiber 2, Carbs 32, Protein 43.

Aromatic Chicken Platter

Preparation time: 10 minutes
Cooking time: 20 minutes
Servings: 4

Ingredients:
- 3 tbsp. olive oil, divided
- 1 yellow bell pepper seeded and sliced
- 1 red bell pepper seeded and sliced
- 1 green bell pepper seeded and sliced
- 1 medium onion, sliced
- 1 lb. boneless, skinless chicken breasts, sliced thinly
- 1 tsp. dried oregano, crushed
- ¼ tsp. garlic powder
- ¼ tsp. ground cumin
- Salt and freshly ground black pepper, to taste
- ¼ cup chicken broth

Directions:
1. In a skillet, heat 1 tbsp. oil over medium-high heat and cook the bell peppers and onion slices for about 4–5 minutes.
2. With a slotted spoon, transfer the peppers mixture onto a plate.

3. In the same skillet, heat the remaining oil over medium-high heat and cook the chicken for about 8 minutes, stirring frequently.
4. Stir in the thyme, spices, salt, black pepper, and broth, and bring to a boil.
5. Add the peppers mixture and stir to combine.
6. Reduce the heat to medium and cook for about 3–5 minutes or until all the liquid is absorbed, stirring occasionally.
7. Serve immediately.

Nutrition: Calories 335, Fat 10, Fiber 2, Carbs 16, Protein 33.

Attractive Scallop Salad

Preparation time: 15 minutes
Cooking time: 6 minutes
Servings: 4
Ingredients:
For Scallops:
- 1¼ lb. fresh sea scallops, side muscles removed
- Salt and freshly ground black pepper, to taste
- 2 tbsp. olive oil
- 1 garlic clove, minced

For Salad:
- 6 cup mixed baby greens
- ¼ cup yellow grape tomatoes, halved
- ¼ cup red grape tomatoes, halved
- 2 tbsp. olive oil
- 2 tbsp. fresh lemon juice
- Salt and freshly ground black pepper, to taste

Directions:
1. Sprinkle the scallops with salt and black pepper evenly.
2. In a large skillet, heat the oil over medium-high heat and cook the scallops for about 2–3 minutes per side.
3. Meanwhile, for the salad: in a bowl, add all ingredients and toss to coat well.
4. Divide the salad onto serving plates.
5. Top each plate with scallops and serve.

Nutrition: Calories 335, Fat 10, Fiber 2, Carbs 16, Protein 33.

Pesto Zucchini Noodles with Grilled Chicken

Preparation time: 10 minutes
Cooking time: 10 minutes
Servings: 4

Ingredients:
- 1/3 cup reduced-fat Italian salad dressing

- ½ cup chopped fresh basil
- ½ cup parmesan cheese, divided
- 1/3 ounces pine nuts
- Cooking spray
- 2 medium zucchinis, spiraled
- 1 ½ pounds grilled boneless chicken breasts, cubed
- 2 cups cherry tomatoes, halved
- ½ teaspoon crushed red pepper flakes

Directions:
1. Combine the salad dressing, basil, half of the parmesan cheese, and pine nuts. Pulse in a blender until smooth.
2. In a lightly greased skillet heated over medium flame; cook the zucchini noodles for 3 minutes. Stir in the pesto and remaining parmesan cheese.
3. Remove from heat and top with chicken, tomatoes, and crushed red pepper flakes.

Nutrition: Calories 335, Fat 10, Fiber 2, Carbs 16, Protein 33.

Citrusy Fruit Salad

Preparation time: 10 minutes
Cooking time: 10 minutes
Servings: 4
Ingredients:
For Salad:
- 4 cup fresh baby arugula
- 1 cup fresh strawberries, hulled and sliced
- 2 oranges, peeled and segmented

For Dressing:
- 2 tbsp. fresh lemon juice
- 2-3 drops liquid stevia
- 2 tsp. extra-virgin olive oil
- Salt and freshly ground black pepper, to taste

Directions:
For salad:
1. In a salad bowl, place all ingredients and mix.

For dressing:
2. place all ingredients in another bowl and beat until well combined.
3. Place dressing on top of the salad and toss to coat well.
4. Serve immediately.

Nutrition: Calories 91, Fat 6, Fiber 2, Carbs 13, Protein 2.

Italian Flair Chicken

Preparation time: 10 minutes
Cooking time: 30 minutes
Servings: 4
Ingredients:

- 2 tbsp. almond flour
- Salt and freshly ground black pepper, to taste
- 4 (4-oz.) skinless, boneless chicken breasts
- 2 tbsp. olive oil
- 6 garlic cloves, chopped
- ¾ lb. fresh mushrooms, sliced
- ¾ cup chicken broth
- ¼ cup balsamic vinegar
- 1 bay leaf
- ¼ tsp. dried thyme

Directions:
1. In a bowl, mix together the flour, salt, and black pepper.
2. Coat the chicken breasts with flour mixture evenly.
3. In a skillet, heat the olive oil over medium-high heat and stir fry chicken for about 3 minutes.
4. Add the garlic and flip the chicken breasts.
5. Spread mushrooms over chicken and cook for about 3 minutes, shaking the skillet frequently.
6. Add the broth, vinegar, bay leaf, and thyme and stir to combine.
7. Reduce the heat to medium-low and simmer, covered for about 10 minutes, flipping chicken occasionally.
8. With a slotted spoon, transfer the chicken onto a warm serving platter, and with a piece of foil, cover to keep warm.
9. Place the pan of sauce over medium-high heat and cook, uncovered for about 7 minutes.
10. Remove the pan from heat and discard the bay leaf.
11. Place mushroom sauce over chicken and serve hot.

Nutrition: Calories 247, Fat 11, Fiber 2, Carbs 6.6, Protein 29.

Cauliflower and Chicken Tzatziki Bowl

Preparation time: 10 minutes
Cooking time: 30 minutes
Servings: 4
Ingredients:

- 5 ½ cups riced cauliflower
- 1 tablespoon parmesan cheese
- ¼ teaspoon salt, divided
- 1-pound boneless chicken breasts cut into strips

- ½ cup grated cucumber
- ½ cup low-fat Greek yogurt, plain
- ½ cup crushed garlic

Directions:

1. Mix together the cauliflower rice, parmesan cheese, and salt. Place in a microwave oven and cook for 1 minute. Set aside.
2. Preheat the oven to 425°F. Season the chicken with salt and bake in the oven for 30 minutes or until golden brown.
3. Meanwhile, place the cucumber, yogurt, and garlic in a bowl. Season with salt and mix until well combined.
4. Assemble by putting the cauliflower rice in a bowl. Prepare four bowls. Top with baked chicken and drizzle with the tzatziki sauce.

Nutrition: Calories 335, Fat 10, Fiber 2, Carbs 16, Protein 33.

Bibimbap Bowls

Preparation time: 10 minutes
Cooking time: 30 minutes
Servings: 4

Ingredients:

- 1 tsp. olive oil
- 5 cups baby spinach
- 1 tsp. toasted sesame oil
- ¼ tsp. salt
- 1 pound 98% lean ground beef
- 2 tbsp. chili garlic sauce
- 1 tbsp. reduced-sodium soy sauce
- 2 cups cauliflower, grated
- 1 cup sliced cucumber
- 4 fried eggs
- ½ cups green onions
- 1 tbsp. sesame seeds

Directions:

1. Heat the oil in a skillet over medium flame. Add the spinach and cook until wilted. Drizzle with sesame seed oil and season with salt. Remove spinach and set aside.
2. Using the same pan, add the beef and cook for 6 minutes while constantly stirring until golden brown. Add the chili garlic sauce and soy sauce and cook for another minute. Remove from heat.
3. Place cauliflower in a microwavable container and heat for 3 minutes until tender.
4. Assemble the bibimbap. Divide the cauliflower rice into 4 containers. Distribute with spinach, beef, cucumber, and egg.
5. Garnish with green onions and sesame seeds.

Nutrition: Calories 415, Fat 10, Fiber 2, Carbs 16, Protein 37.

Chicken Fajita Platter

Preparation time: 10 minutes
Cooking time: 25 minutes
Servings: 4
Ingredients:

- 1 lb. boneless, skinless chicken breasts cut into thin strips
- ½ of green bell pepper seeded and cut into strips
- ½ of red bell pepper seeded and cut into strips
- 1 medium onion, sliced
- 2 tbsp. olive oil
- ½ tsp. dried oregano
- 2 tsp. chili powder
- 1½ tsp. ground cumin
- 1 tsp. garlic powder
- Salt, to taste

Directions:
1. Preheat the oven to 400°F.
2. In a bowl, add all the ingredients and mix well.
3. Place the chicken mixture into a 9x13-inch baking dish and spread in an even layer.
4. Bake for about 20–25 minutes or until chicken is done completely.
5. Serve hot.

Nutrition: Calories 335, Fat 10, Fiber 2, Carbs 16, Protein 33.

Broccoli Taco Bowl

Preparation time: 15 minutes
Cooking time: 12 minutes
Servings: 1
Ingredients:

- 4 oz. lean ground beef
- 1 cup broccoli, cut into bite-sized pieces
- 2 tbsp. chicken broth
- ¼ cup tomatoes, chopped
- ¼ tsp. onion powder
- ¼ tsp. garlic powder
- Pinch of red pepper flakes
- Salt, to taste
- 1 oz. low-fat cheddar cheese

Directions:
1. Heat a lightly greased skillet over medium heat and cook the beef for about 8–10 minutes or until browned completely.
2. Meanwhile, in a microwave-safe bowl, place the broccoli and broth.

3. With a plastic wrap, cover the bowl and microwave for about 4 minutes.
4. Remove from the microwave and set aside.
5. Drain the grease from the skillet.
6. Add the tomatoes, garlic powder, onion powder, red pepper flakes, and salt and stir to combine well.
7. Add the broccoli and toss to coat well.
8. Remove from the heat and transfer the beef mixture into a serving bowl.
9. Top with cheddar cheese and serve.

Nutrition: Calories 375, Fat 17, Fiber 2, Carbs 9, Protein 54

Summertime Dinner Chicken

Preparation time: 17 minutes
Cooking time: 15 minutes
Servings: 6
Ingredients:

- 2 tbsp. olive oil, divided
- 1½ lb. skinless, boneless chicken breasts, cut into bite-sized pieces
- Salt and freshly ground black pepper, to taste
- 2 garlic cloves, minced
- 1½ lb. yellow squash, sliced
- 2 tbsp. fresh lemon juice
- 1 tsp. fresh lemon zest, grated finely
- 2 tbsp. fresh parsley, minced

Directions:

1. In a large skillet, heat 1 tbsp. oil over medium heat and stir fry chicken for about 6–8 minutes or until golden brown from all sides.
2. Transfer the chicken onto a plate.
3. In the same skillet, heat remaining oil over medium heat and sauté garlic for about 1 minute.
4. Add the squash slices and cook for about 5–6 minutes.
5. Stir in the chicken and cook for about 2 minutes.
6. Stir in the lemon juice, zest, and parsley and remove from heat.
7. Serve hot.

Nutrition: Calories 335, Fat 10, Fiber 2, Carbs 16, Protein 33.

Authentic Chinese Chicken

Preparation time: 10 minutes
Cooking time: 10 minutes
Servings: 6
Ingredients:

- 3 garlic cloves, minced
- ½ cup fresh orange juice

- 1 tbsp. apple cider vinegar
- 2 tbsp. low-sodium soy sauce
- ¼ tsp. ground ginger
- ¼ tsp. ground cinnamon
- Freshly ground black pepper, to taste
- 2 lb. skinless, bone-in chicken thighs
- 1/3 cup scallion, sliced

Directions:

1. To marinate in a large bowl, mix together all ingredients except for chicken thighs and scallion.
2. Add the chicken thighs and coat with marinade generously.
3. Cover the bowl and refrigerate to marinate for about 4 hours.
4. Remove the chicken from the bowl, reserving marinade.
5. Heat a lightly greased large non-stick skillet over medium-high heat and cook the chicken thighs for about 5–6 minutes or till golden brown.
6. Flip the side and cook for about 4 minutes.
7. Stir in the reserved marinade and bring to a boil.
8. Reduce the heat to medium-low and cook, covered for about 6–8 minutes or until sauce becomes thick.
9. Stir in the scallion and remove from the heat.
10. Serve hot.

Nutrition: Calories 205, Fat 6, Fiber 2, Carbs 3.6, Protein 34.

CHAPTER 13:
Fueling Recipes

Pumpkin Pie Trail Mix
Preparation time: 10 minutes
Cooking time: 30 minutes
Servings: 3
Ingredients:
- ½ tbsp. pumpkin seed kernels
- ½ tbsp. slivered almonds
- ¼ tsp. pumpkin pie spice
- ½ tbsp. Walden Maple Walnut or Pancake Syrup
- 1 sachet Optavia Olive Oil & Sea Salt Popcorn

Directions:
1. Mix the syrup with pumpkin pie spice.
2. Get a quart-sized small bowl or resealable plastic bag to combine the pumpkin seed kernels, silvered almonds, Olive Oil & Sea Salt Popcorn. Trickle with syrup mixture.
3. Mix gently or toss together to make the popcorn evenly coat.

Nutrition: Calories 95, Fat 5, Fiber 6, Carbs 5, Protein 4.

Chocolate Popsicle
Preparation time: 10 minutes
Cooking time: 2 minutes
Servings: 4
Ingredients:
- 4 oz. unsweetened chocolate, chopped
- 6 drops liquid stevia
- 1 1/2 cups heavy cream

Directions:
1. Add heavy cream into the microwave-safe bowl and microwave until just begins the boiling.
2. Add chocolate into the heavy cream and set aside for 5 minutes.
3. Add liquid stevia into the heavy cream mixture and stir until chocolate is melted.
4. Pour mixture into the Popsicle molds and place in freezer for 4 hours or until set.
5. Serve and enjoy it.

Nutrition: Calories 155, Fat 15, Fiber 4, Carbs 4, Protein 3.

Tropical Chia Seed Pudding

Preparation time: 10 minutes
Cooking time: 5 minutes
Servings: 2
Ingredients:

- ½ tsp. lemon zest (optional)
- 1 cup refrigerated unsweetened coconut milk
- ¼ cup chia seeds
- 2 sachets Optavia Chia Bliss Smoothie

Directions:

1. Get a mixing bowl to combine all of the ingredients and stir till they are well blended. Transfer the mixture inside a glass container or jar and keep refrigerated overnight.

Nutrition: Calories 95, Fat 5, Fiber 6, Carbs 5, Protein 4.

Blueberry Muffins

Preparation time: 10 minutes
Cooking time: 30 minutes
Servings: 4
Ingredients:

- 2 eggs
- 1/2 cup fresh blueberries
- 1 cup heavy cream
- 2 cups almond flour
- 1/4 tsp. lemon zest
- 1/2 tsp. lemon extract
- 1 tsp. baking powder
- 5 drops stevia
- 1/4 cup butter, melted

Directions:

1. Preheat the oven to 350°F. Line muffins tin with cupcake liners and set aside.
2. Add eggs into the bowl and whisk until mix.
3. Add remaining ingredients and mix to combine.
4. Pour mixture into the prepared muffin tin and bake for 25 minutes.
5. Serve and enjoy it.

Nutrition: Calories 195, Fat 5, Fiber 6, Carbs 5, Protein 4.

Delicious Brownie Bites

Preparation time: 10 minutes
Cooking time: 20 minutes
Servings: 12
Ingredients:
- 1/4 cup unsweetened chocolate chips
- 1/4 cup unsweetened cocoa powder
- 1 cup pecans, chopped
- 1/2 cup almond butter
- 1/2 tsp. vanilla
- 1/4 cup monk fruit sweetener
- 1/8 tsp. pink salt

Directions:
1. Add pecans, sweetener, vanilla, almond butter, cocoa powder, and salt into the food processor and process until well combined.
2. Transfer brownie mixture into the large bowl. Add chocolate chips and fold well.
3. Make small round shape balls from brownie mixture and place onto a baking tray.
4. Place in the freezer for 20 minutes.
5. Serve and enjoy it.

Nutrition: Calories 155, Fat 15, Fiber 4, Carbs 4, Protein 3.

Chocolate Bars

Preparation time: 10 minutes
Cooking time: 30 minutes
Servings: 12
Ingredients:
- 15 oz. cream cheese, softened
- 15 oz. unsweetened dark chocolate
- 1 tsp. vanilla
- 10 drops liquid stevia

Directions:
1. Grease an 8-inch square dish and set aside.
2. Melt chocolate in a saucepan over low heat.
3. Add stevia and vanilla and stir well.
4. Remove pan from heat and set aside.
5. Add cream cheese into the blender and blend until smooth.
6. Add melted chocolate mixture into the cream cheese and blend until just combined.
7. Transfer mixture into the prepared dish and spread evenly, and place it in the refrigerator until firm.
8. Slice and serve.

Nutrition: Calories 235, Fat 25, Fiber 6, Carbs 7, Protein 6.

Coconut Colada

Preparation time: 10 minutes
Cooking time: 10 minutes
Servings: 1
Ingredients:
- ½ cup ice
- ¼ tsp. rum extract
- 2 tbsp. shredded unsweetened coconut with 2 extra teaspoons for topping
- 6 oz. diet ginger ale
- 6 oz. unsweetened original coconut milk
- 1 sachet Optavia Essential Creamy Vanilla Shake

Directions:
1. Get a blender to combine all of the ingredients and blend until they become smooth and icy.
2. Get 2 pina colada glasses and divide the smooth mixture between them before topping with the remaining shredded coconut. You should serve instantly.

Nutrition: Calories 95, Fat 5, Fiber 6, Carbs 5, Protein 4.

Dark Chocolate Berry Dessert Parfait

Preparation time: 10 minutes
Cooking time: 10 minutes
Servings: 4
Ingredients:
- 2/3 oz. of sliced almonds
- 1 Optavia Chocolate Cherry Ganache Bar
- 1–2 packets zero-calorie sugar substitute
- 1 tablespoon unsweetened cocoa powder
- ¼ cup strawberry-flavored, light cream cheese
- 1 ½ cups plain, non-fat Greek yogurt

Directions:
1. Put all of the ingredients inside a blender and blend on high heat for about 1–2 minutes or until they are well mixed.

Nutrition: Calories 235, Fat 25, Fiber 1, Carbs 8, Protein 9.

Vanilla Avocado Popsicles

Preparation time: 10 minutes
Cooking time: 20 minutes
Servings: 6
Ingredients:
- 2 avocadoes
- 1 tsp. vanilla
- 1 cup almond milk

- 1 tsp. liquid stevia
- 1/2 cup unsweetened cocoa powder

Directions:
1. Add all ingredients into the blender and blend until smooth.
2. Pour blended mixture into the Popsicle molds and place in the freezer until set.
3. Serve and enjoy it.

Nutrition: Calories 135, Fat 12, Fiber 4, Carbs 7, Protein 3.

Pumpkin Pie Frappe

Preparation time: 10 minutes
Cooking time: 30 minutes
Servings: 4
Ingredients:
- 2 tablespoons of pressurized whipped topping
- 1/8 teaspoon of pumpkin pie spice
- ½ cup of ice
- 4 oz. of strong brewed coffee should be chilled
- 4 oz. of unsweetened cashew milk or vanilla almond
- 1 sachet of Optavia Essential Spiced Gingerbread

Directions:
1. Combine the pumpkin pie spice, ice, brewed coffee, cashew milk, or vanilla, and spiced Gingerbread inside a blender and blend them until they become smooth.
2. Then, top with the whipped topping before serving.

Nutrition: Calories 155, Fat 15, Fiber 4, Carbs 4, Protein 3.

Boo-Nila Shake

Preparation time: 10 minutes
Cooking time: 30 minutes
Servings: 4
Ingredients:
- 2 tbsp. pressurized whipped topping
- ½ cup ice
- 8 oz. unsweetened cashew milk or vanilla almond
- 1 sachet Optavia Essential Creamy Vanilla Shake

Directions:
1. Get a blender to combine the ice, cashew milk or vanilla almond, and Creamy Vanilla Shake and blend everything together till they become smooth.
2. You can use a black permanent marker to decorate a plastic or glass, cup or mason jar and have a ghost face on it (This is optional).

3. Then, top with the whipped topping before serving.

Nutrition: Calories 95, Fat 5, Fiber 6, Carbs 5, Protein 4.

Chia Pudding

Preparation time: 10 minutes
Cooking time: 20 minutes
Servings: 2
Ingredients:
- 4 tbsp. chia seeds
- 1 cup unsweetened coconut milk
- 1/2 cup raspberries

Directions:
1. Add raspberry and coconut milk into a blender and blend until smooth.
2. Pour mixture into the glass jar.
3. Add chia seeds in a jar and stir well.
4. Seal the jar with a lid and shake well and place it in the refrigerator for 3 hours.
5. Serve chilled and enjoy it.

Nutrition: Calories 395, Fat 5, Fiber 6, Carbs 5, Protein 4.

Richly Tasty Crepe

Preparation time: 10 minutes
Cooking time: 10 minutes
Servings: 1
Ingredients:
- 1 packet Medifast Chocolate Chip Pancakes
- ¼ cup water
- ¼ cup part-skim ricotta cheese
- ½ packet stevia powder
- 1/8 tsp. vanilla extract
- 1 tsp. sugar-free chocolate syrup

Directions:
1. In a bowl, add the pancake and water and mix well.
2. Heat a lightly greased skillet over medium heat.
3. Place the mixture and spread it in a thin circle.
4. Cook for about 1–2 minutes per side or until golden brown.
5. Remove from the heat and place the crepe onto a plate.
6. In a small bowl, add the ricotta cheese, stevia, and vanilla extract and mix until well combined.
7. Place the mixture inside the crepe.
8. Drizzle with chocolate syrup and serve.

Nutrition: Calories 185, Fat 10, Fiber 4, Carbs 16, Protein 19.

Peanut Butter Coconut Popsicle

Preparation time: 10 minutes
Cooking time: 20 minutes
Servings: 14
Ingredients:
- 1/2 cup peanut butter
- 1 tsp. liquid stevia
- 2 cans unsweetened coconut milk

Directions:
1. Add all ingredients into the blender and blend until smooth.
2. Pour mixture into the Popsicle molds and place in the freezer for 4 hours or until set.
3. Serve and enjoy it.

Nutrition: Calories 155, Fat 15, Fiber 4, Carbs 4, Protein 3

Smooth Peanut Butter Cream

Preparation time: 10 minutes
Cooking time: 30 minutes
Servings: 8
Ingredients:
- 1/4 cup peanut butter
- 4 overripe bananas, chopped
- 1/3 cup cocoa powder
- 1/4 tsp vanilla extract
- 1/8 tsp salt

Directions:
1. Add all ingredients into the blender and blend until smooth.
2. Serve immediately and enjoy it.

Nutrition: Calories 155, Fat 15, Fiber 4, Carbs 4, Protein 3.

Avocado Pudding

Preparation time: 10 minutes
Cooking time: 20 minutes
Servings: 4
Ingredients:
- 2 ripe avocados, peeled, pitted, and cut into pieces
- 1 tbsp. fresh lime juice
- 14 oz. can coconut milk
- 2 tsp. liquid stevia
- 2 tsp. vanilla

Directions:

1. Add all ingredients into the blender and blend until smooth.
2. Serve immediately and enjoy it.

Nutrition: Calories 315, Fat 10, Fiber 4, Carbs 6, Protein 3.

Skinny Peppermint Mocha

Preparation time: 10 minutes
Cooking time: 5 minutes
Servings: 1
Ingredients:

- Pinch of cinnamon
- 2 tablespoon of pressurized whipped topping
- ¼ teaspoon of peppermint extract
- ¼ cup of unsweetened cashew milk or vanilla almond, should be warmed
- 6 oz. of freshly brewed coffee
- 1 Sachet of Optavia Essential Velvety Hot Chocolate

Directions:

1. Get a coffee cup or mug to combine the cashew milk or vanilla almond, brewed coffee, and Velvety Hot Chocolate and stir everything together until the Velvety Hot Chocolate dissolves.
2. Top it with the whipped topping and spread cinnamon at the top.

Nutrition: Calories 155, Fat 15, Fiber 4, Carbs 4, Protein 3.

Pumpkin Balls

Preparation time: 10 minutes
Cooking time: 10 minutes
Servings: 14
Ingredients:

- 1 cup almond butter
- 5 drops liquid stevia
- 2 tbsp. coconut flour
- 2 tbsp. pumpkin puree
- 1 tsp. pumpkin pie spice

Directions:

1. In a large bowl, mix together pumpkin puree and almond butter until well combined.
2. Add liquid stevia, pumpkin pie spice, and coconut flour and mix well.
3. Make small balls from the mixture and place onto a baking tray.
4. Place in the freezer for 1 hour.
5. Serve and enjoy it.

Nutrition: Calories 55, Fat 15, Fiber 4, Carbs 4, Protein 2.

Conclusion

If you are interested in trying it, consider working with an expert registered dietitian who can help you make sure you are staying adequately nourished while you are striving to reach your desired weight.

For the duration of the most desirable weight 5&1 plan, you eat 5 Fueling in line with the day, plus a low carb Lean and Green meal and an elective low carb snack.

While the initial 5&1 Plan is reasonably restrictive, the 3&3 protection segment allows for a greater variety of food and fewer processed snacks, which can also make weight loss and adherence simpler to maintain for a long time.

However, the diet is costly, repetitive, and doesn't accommodate all nutritional wishes. What's extra, extended calorie limit may also result in nutrient deficiencies and different potential health issues.

The bottom line is that the Optavia weight loss plan promotes weight loss via low-calorie prepackaged meals; low carb homemade food, and personalized coaching; at the same time, as this system promotes quick-time period weight and fat loss, similarly research is wanted to assess whether it encourages the everlasting way of life adjustments needed for long-time period achievement.

We all know how hard life is for people who are overweight. And if you've read this book and have come this far, you must be dealing with a weight problem. At this moment of your journey, it is crucial for you to recognize that you've overcome the hardest task, i.e., the first dreadful step towards health and wellbeing. Please remember that this alone is a commendable feat. And whoever survives the first step can definitely survive the rest and come out of the other side thinner, stronger, wiser, happier, and overall better.

If you need motivation or if you doubt yourself before joining the amazing Optavia Community, rest assured that this is the right thing to do for your health and wellness. The Optavia coaches are always there for you to support you, guide you, and streamline your journey towards personal growth. Never be shy to reach out to them if you need any kind of help.

Do not treat it as a "diet" because clean eating is supposed to be a lifestyle and permanent change and not just a trend. Having said that, forgive yourself if you ever make a mistake along the way. Remember, the journey of a thousand miles still begins with just a single step indeed. So, stand tall, be confident, and just go ahead each day with your ideal vision of yourself in your mind moving a bit closer to your goals every day.

Thank you.

www.ingramcontent.com/pod-product-compliance
Lightning Source LLC
Chambersburg PA
CBHW080608170426
43209CB00007B/1373